NANNETTE L. KAMIEN, CFP®, MBA

Crazy College Money

Make Smart College Money Choices – Without The Crazy

Edited by: Erika Brucia

First edition

ISBN: 978-1-088502-35-8

This book was professionally typeset on Reedsy.
Find out more at reedsy.com

For My Mom,
Who Always Believed in the Value of an Education

Contents

III   Make Good Choices

Intro

There is no Financial Aid Fairy. You'd be surprised how many people act like there is. What I've learned over the last 4 years of helping clients figure out how to pay for college is that hope is a popular strategy parents have when they begin the college admissions process. Hope is not a strategy I want you to use.

I'm not sure why hope is so popular. People seem to be able to make rational decisions when buying a house. Usually the purchase budget is the first thing they consider. The budget guides the process. When they apply for a mortgage, there's an underwriter using real numbers to decide if a bank believes they can pay back the loan. There's an appraiser who decides if the house is worth what they are paying.

Why isn't that the case with paying for college? There are families who go through the entire college admissions process without even considering money. They get the first bill during the summer prior to their child's freshman year, and THEY DON'T KNOW HOW THEY PLAN TO PAY IT! This blows my mind.

By the way, it's not like a slightly unaffordable mortgage payment. It can be a $20,000 or $30,000 PER SEMESTER bill. Obviously, the earlier people come to me, the more I can help them. But there's no Financial Aid Fairy that is going to wave her wand and make a $30,000 bill go away.

I've seen some crazy stuff in my time helping parents whose kids are getting ready to go to college. I recently heard of a family who sent their kid to college and didn't get the meal plan because they couldn't afford it! Hunger is a growing problem on college campuses, as is homelessness. Students can't focus on studying because they don't have anywhere to sleep and don't have anything to eat. How does this make sense?

But who the heck am I to tell you what to do during this emotional time in your life?

I'm writing this book because I'm passionate about keeping regular people from making horrible financial decisions about college that can wreck their (and their kids') financial lives forever. There's no way I can help everyone that needs it through my financial planning practice, so I'm trying to reach the masses by writing this book.

If you're a parent who wants to learn everything you need to know to make smart decisions about paying for college, this book is for you. It doesn't matter if you have a senior getting ready to fill out applications, or your kids just entered middle school. It's never too early or late to educate yourself.

My story isn't unique. I borrowed money to pay for my undergraduate degree (a B.A. in Spanish), and then borrowed money to pay for my first year of law school. When I realized there was no legal job of my dreams after that year, I went back for more undergraduate education in computer science (right before the dot com bust). Yep, you guessed it, I borrowed money to do that too. After 3 semesters more, I decided that I knew enough to get a job and start paying my bills. I was lucky enough to get one with Motorola that paid a good salary. Subsequently, I could pay off my student loans because I made money selling my first condo during the real estate bubble. I didn't really have a plan for all of that.

I did a couple of things right. I went to undergrad at a school that gave me a LOT of financial aid. In fact, I chose that school because it was CHEAPER than going to the state school up the street. I got a scholarship for tuition for that first year of law school, so my loans that year were only for living expenses. Then when I did end up attending that state school up the street for three semesters of computer science, I lived in a cheap apartment and waitressed part time to help pay the bills.

I spent the first 15 years of my career in Information Technology jobs, and during that time borrowed another $100k to go to an expensive school for an MBA. I thought that would solve all my problems with my lack of job satisfaction. It didn't. Getting a fancy MBA does not make you like your career more.

Five years ago, I made the jump to become a financial planner serving regular, mid-career people like me. I started my own firm so I wouldn't have to focus only on working with affluent seniors who needed their investments managed, like most firms do. I wanted my services and fees to be straightforward, easy to understand, and affordable for the average Jane and Joe.

What I found out in working with parents of kids going to college is that many were caught up in the college marketing machine. They were convinced there was a short list of well-ranked schools and if their child didn't attend one of those, their kid's life would be ruined. They were carrying emotional baggage from their own college experience. They had some parenting guilt, and pressure to keep up with the Joneses. All of this while there's a lack of education around paying for college, and a financial aid system in place that is not meant to work in their favor.

You're going to be smarter than that. You've proven that by buying this book.

In case you haven't heard, there's a student loan crisis.

Borrowers owe more than $1.5 TRILLION in student loans.

What that big number masks is that there are real families borrowing way more than they can afford, more than they can ever pay back, and for almost everyone, it's debt they can't even get away from by declaring bankruptcy.

Worse, money is being borrowed by people who will never graduate and never reap the supposed benefits of a college degree. It's leaving them deeper in the hole than when they started.

It's affecting the economy because graduates are having trouble finding jobs that will pay their bills and loan payments. They can't move out of their parents' houses, buy houses of their own, or get married and start families. I'm going to help you stop the crazy right in its tracks.

"Investing" in a college education has always been touted by financial gurus as "good debt" as far back as I can remember. There's evidence the payoff for an undergraduate degree is shrinking. For some degrees and for some people – especially ones who fail to graduate – there isn't a payoff any longer. All of this needs to be considered when making decisions about where to go for college, how much to pay, and what to major in. We will cover those topics in this book.

We will also deal with that emotional stuff I mentioned a while back. We'll start with that, in fact. Because that's the root of where all the crazy comes from. You need to know if you're the crazy one here. You will need to recognize the signs of becoming the crazy one.

I'm also going to give you the basic information on financial aid that you must learn to be successful doing this yourself. I see a lot of questions in Facebook forums I'm part of (in fact, I'm an admin of two – Ask the Experts About Paying for College, and Crazy College Money), that show a lack of understanding of the financial aid process. It's ok. You aren't expected to know this stuff going in, but you should feel empowered to learn it. That's where this book comes in.

Sometimes I'm going to be able to give you answers and direction. Sometimes I'll only be able to tell you what pieces of data you're looking for, along with the right questions to ask. I may not even be able to tell you who to ask, but I'm hopefully going to steer you away from asking some people you may not be able to trust.

There are a lot of so-called college financial consultants out there. Everyone from people you can pay to fill out the FAFSA for you, to ones who are selling you insurance policies you don't need to "beat the financial aid system". There might be those who tell you to transfer guardianship of your child or get a divorce to get more financial aid. I don't do any of these: I work with families one on one to help them figure out the right strategy for them, in the context of their comprehensive financial plan. I'm a fiduciary, with a legal obligation to give families advice in their best interests only. I'm not tied to recommending certain solutions and strategies because they benefit me. So I'm here to help you choose the best option for YOUR family.

Figuring out your strategy is on the one hand easy enough that this book will get you 95% of the way there, and difficult enough that many CPAs and CFP®s don't have the expertise to give you the right advice. My goal is to give everyone who needs it the confidence to do it themselves, and to know when they might need more help. You can recognize your emotional influences, learn about financial aid, have the hard conversations with your kids, and get out of this process without making dumb money decisions. Your kids will thank you when they don't have to support you in your old age. Your future "you" will thank you.

Finally, there will be tough love in this book. I am not of the opinion that your child is a fragile flower that deserves to go to the school of his/her dreams regardless of the impact on your finances. I am also not of the opinion that you should be able to avoid these tough decisions and conversations and whine about how it's not fair. It isn't fair. Life isn't fair. The sooner you and your child accept that, the easier this process becomes.

There are schools you can't afford. There are schools your child can't get into. Buckle up for a wild ride where you learn what you need to know and do to keep the crazy out of paying for college.

I

Emotions and College Money

1

High School is Crazy Today

I'm lucky. My kids aren't in high school yet. Every day I see articles about the pressure high school kids are under. I read about how depression and anxiety rates are skyrocketing. It seems that kids are overworked, tired, and caught up in the rat race to be the perfect student.

A lot of it is because of parents who are afraid that their child will be left behind if they don't get into the perfect college. Some of these parents are willing to do whatever it takes to send their kid to the school of their dreams.

There is not a guaranteed formula like A + B + C = the perfect life.

Let your kid enjoy high school. If they want to take advanced classes, let them. Don't force them. If they want to play sports, let them. Don't force them. If they want to be involved in activities, let them. Don't force them. Chasing the "perfect" college resume is futile, because schools have varying definitions of the perfect student. Even perfect students get denied admission.

There is a lot of uncertainty in the world today. What I do know is that high school is likely the last time in their lives your kids will have the opportunity for less responsibility. Let them enjoy it. Kids with "perfect" applications get rejected from Harvard all the time. "Mediocre" students graduate from mediocre colleges and are happy and successful in life. The real "perfect" college fit is a place your child can fit academically, socially, and financially, not the #1 ranked school on some media website.

2

Your College Money Philosophy

I'm going to start this book off by telling you that paying for college is first an emotional choice and then a financial one, which you might think is strange. After all, I'm a financial planner and much of what I will be covering relates to your finances.

But I want you to dig deep inside and get in touch with your feelings and experiences for a second. We'll get to the numbers shortly (like the next chapter). This is where some of the tough love is going to come in, so brace yourself. You're going to have to ask yourself if YOU are the crazy in this situation.

Like I said in the intro, I've seen crazy stuff in my practice. Parents can be completely irrational when it comes to making the college decision. There is usually something going on behind the scenes that is driving this behavior. Sometimes I can recognize it and get them to acknowledge it. I can't always talk them off the cliff, though.

I'm going to start you off with giving you work to do. Get out a piece of paper or open a notes app on your phone. Write down these questions as you work through them and especially your answers. I'm serious, write down your answers.

When you're done, laminate it and stick it on your refrigerator or your bathroom mirror. Keep it there during your child's junior and senior years of high school. You will need it to remind you of what sanity looks like.

There are going to be times during this process where you are ready to throw all rationality to the side and make dumb decisions. Your answers below may be all that's standing between you and a huge financial mistake.

Developing Your College Money Philosophy

What was your college money experience?

I find that there are a couple of typical money experiences parents have had in their college journey. Do any of these resonate with you?

The Generous Parents

Some parents had their whole college experience paid for and never worried about money. These parents usually either want to provide that experience for their kids, or the opposite: they want their kids to have some skin in the game and work for it. Which one are you?

Those Who Worked

Others had to work through college. Here the reactions are usually two-fold as well. Either the parents want their kid to have to work to pay for college, or they want to remove that burden from them and pay their way for them. Where do you stand on work?

Those Who Borrowed

The third most popular story I hear is about student loans. Either the parents had to borrow a lot, and it may have affected their ability to save and they wish they hadn't done it. Or, they borrowed minimally and are glad that it taught them to be responsible and helped them build a credit history. Some people have sworn off debt forever because of their college money experience. Where do you stand on borrowing to pay for college?

The Budgeters

There are parents who got an amount from their family that they could contribute, and they were expected to choose schools wisely and make up the difference with work and loans. Is this you?

The Parents Who Didn't go to College

One other type of family is where one or both parents didn't attend college. If this is you, you'll need to dig into why. Could your family not afford it? Was there not the expectation that you attend? Do you regret it or feel like you turned out just fine?

Emotions get high when you can't afford to pay for school, or you don't want to. You lose sleep about not being able to provide for your child. Your child may have grown up with the expectation you will pay for school. They may have a dream school in mind, and it's quite upsetting if that option isn't available.

If you worked through college, you may not realize that it's impossible to work your way through school like you did in the past. The cost of attending school is so high compared to what your child can earn to pay for it, that they don't have the same options you did. You may be disappointed that your child will miss out on an experience you feel built your character.

You may be aware of the student loan debt crisis. You may know that graduates are leaving school with ever increasing piles of debt that delays their ability to get established on their own. It's more important than ever that you help your child make responsible borrowing decisions.

If your family set a budget and made you stick to it, you may want to plan a similar budget for your child or children. Others of you may have resented that you didn't have more choices, and want to send your child wherever they want to go.

All these experiences tie into how you view paying for college for your child. Write yours down.

What was your spouse/partner's experience?

It's rare where I get a couple who both had the same college money experience. When I start asking these questions and the answers come out, they realize they've never talked about this period in their lives. They recognize they are going into the college process with different assumptions that may trip them up come decision time.

When you take into consideration all the different experiences that parents bring to the table regarding paying for college, it makes sense that emotions play a big role in the college funding decisions families make.

If one of you had a generous parent, and your spouse worked through college, you may need to discuss how you want to approach paying for college. If one of you borrowed and regretted it, while the other had a budget and borrowed responsibly to fill the gap, you will need to reconcile these experiences into a family plan.

The biggest tip is to have this conversation now, before you even start talking about college with your children. Don't wait until you're reviewing the list of schools they want to apply to.

What are your child's college money expectations?

There's a disconnect between the number of kids who think their parents will pay for whatever college they want to attend versus the number of parents who CAN pay. I've got a whole chapter about having the college money talk. Right now, it's time to face what their expectations are TODAY, before you might have to go about changing them. It's a very popular expectation in our society that kids should only have to worry about getting into the best schools that they can, while parents should figure out how to pay for it.

I'm not sure where this expectation comes from, but it's important to nip it in the bud early. I'm a big proponent of having discussions with kids about paying for college starting in middle school (or younger). Set their expectations early.

How do you feel about student loans and borrowing to pay for school?

Students (and parents!) are borrowing at higher levels than ever before. Average balances are going up, delinquencies are up, and most agree that the economy is being weighed down by all of this.

Your experience with borrowing usually has a big influence on how you answer this question. If you borrowed responsibly and have paid off your loans, you may think it's no big deal. If you're still paying your loans while reading this book, you may have a different opinion. It's important to write down whether you view borrowing as a necessary evil, a smart way for students to have skin in the game, out of the question, or something else entirely.

How do you feel about your child working to help pay for school?

It astounds me how few teenagers have jobs these days. Regardless of why that is, someday your child will need to learn a work ethic and figure out the value of earning a dollar. Summer jobs between academic years are one way to contribute. Part-time jobs during school are another.

On the other hand, just because you worked your way through school doesn't mean they can. The economics don't work anymore because the hourly wage hasn't kept up with the cost of attending college. But studies show that a certain amount of work during school helps students succeed academically, while too much is a detriment.

What do you think the role of scholarships should be?

Did you earn scholarships when you went to college? If they were based on academics or sports, you might have that same expectation for your child. Maybe they've been playing travel sports forever in the hope that they get a full ride for college. There's more information about scholarships later, but right here is where you need to write down your beliefs and emotions around scholarships.

How do you feel about getting a second job, spending less now, retiring later, spending less in retirement, selling your house or other assets or making other sacrifices?

What are you willing to do? For most parents, they can't just write a check when the college bill comes. There are trade-offs that need to be made. Deciding what those are ahead of time is an important step in not letting the crazy take over. Some parents may be willing to get an extra job while their kids are in college. Some may be willing to sell their house and downsize. I'm not here to judge the trade-offs you are willing to make, but just get you to understand that there ARE trade-offs. You will need to prioritize which ones you might be willing to make. Equally important is knowing which ones are off the table.

Finalizing Your College Money Philosophy

These questions and answers may bring up painful thoughts. They may bring up emotions about your past, and your feelings about what kind of parent you ought to be. They might make you feel inadequate. Or they might make you feel proud of what

11

you've overcome and what you've instilled in your child.

The important part is to think about them, and WRITE DOWN THE ANSWERS. Talk to your spouse/partner about them. Talk to your child about them and share your stories – good and bad. They will thank you for it later.

Finally, write down your College Money Philosophy. It should sound something like:

> *I want my child to be able to go to college debt-free and graduate in 4 years with a degree that will help them get a good job. I'm willing to help them make smart choices to get there. I'm willing to let them live at home, while they go to school, to save money and I will contribute $5,000 per year toward their tuition. I'm not willing to jeopardize our family's financial future by borrowing to help them attend a school that isn't in budget.*

Or maybe like this:

> *I would like my child to have a similar experience going to college as I did. I would like them to earn scholarships, attend a small, private school and live on campus, and take out a small amount of student loans so they have some skin in the game. I'm willing to work a few more years before I retire so that I can replace my retirement contributions that I will be suspending while I pay out of pocket for college. I'm not willing to jeopardize our family's financial future by borrowing to help them attend a school that isn't in budget.*

And, although I'm not judging your trade-offs, it shouldn't be:

I am willing to do whatever it takes to send my child to the school of their dreams. I am willing to sell my house, borrow money I don't know how I'll pay back, drain my retirement accounts, get divorced, rack up credit card debt, and work until I drop to make this happen.

That would be crazy.

3

Your College Money Reality

O k. We got that out of the way for the moment. This chapter's going to be all about the reality of the numbers. For some of you, this may be scarier than the emotions. You're going to have to get over it. Regardless of what your philosophy on college money was in the previous exercise, your wallet may not let you follow it. Let's look at reality.

Schools want to know about your finances if they are going to give you any of their money. Lenders want to know too. You might as well get a handle on them yourself, first, before you ever have to share anything during the financial aid process.

There's no need to judge yourself. It is what it is.

Some people complain about having to share their family finances with schools and the federal government. That's fine. You aren't required to share anything with anyone if you want to write a check for the full cost to attend college for 4 or more years for each of your children. Schools will be happy to cash those checks. If you need any help, however, you're going to have to open the "books" of your family finances.

Start with your income

When the government asks the schools to report data on finan-cial aid, they break income into 5 different buckets: under $30k, $30-$48k, $48-$75k, $75-$110k, and $110k +. I ask you to start here because your financial resources and strategies to pay for college are going to be very different depending upon your income bucket. But regardless of where your income falls, THERE'S NO REASON TO PAY MORE THAN NECESSARY for college.

If you have high income and can write a check for the full cost of attendance at whatever school your child chooses, that's great. But don't you want a discount? You need to understand the process, go through the emotion questions to decide what you WANT to do, and get the best deal possible by picking the right school.

If you're in a lower income bucket, it's super important to understand the process and make the right decisions. Likely you want to make life better for your child and you think college might be the ticket. But you also don't want to make your precarious finances worse, and I'm here to help you.

The income the financial aid process cares about is a little different than what you see in your paycheck, but for now we're going to ignore that. For right now, just write down your income, where it comes from, and get familiar with your tax return to know what is taxed and what isn't.

Wait. Did I just say tax return? Yep. Dig it out and look at it. Either you will need to transfer numbers from your return into the financial aid applications, or connect to the IRS Data Retrieval Tool (DRT) to pull the numbers systematically during the financial aid process. We will talk more about this process later.

Assess your expenses

This part is just for you because schools don't care about your expenses. They really don't (for the most part, unless they ask about special circumstances, but we'll talk about that during the financial aid chapter). They don't care about your mortgage, your car payment, or the high cost of living where you are. They don't care if you're still paying your own student loans, what your cell phone costs, or how much you pay in private school tuition.

This is where I see a lot of parents lose it. They've spent their adult lives trying to make ends meet. They're doing the best they can. They have bills to pay and there's not much left over at the end of the month. And colleges don't CARE? This is the first sign that the college financial aid process is NOT about how much you can afford, with schools stepping in to help you pay for the rest. They are in it for them, not you.

You need to dig into your expenses for two reasons: to figure out if you have money left over from your income, and to figure out if you have areas where you can cut expenses so you can have more left over to pay as you go.

Your emergency fund

Don't have one? Go scrounge around in your car and your couch cushions for 5 bucks and start one now. I'm serious. Before you can even think about paying for college, there are a couple of non-negotiables you need to have in place with your family finances. The emergency fund is numero uno.

16

Rule of thumb tells you that you should have at least 3-6 months of basic expenses saved in an emergency fund to consider it fully funded. To some people, that number is preposterous. That's ok. I'm not here to argue about what the right emergency fund number is. I'm here to tell you that if you don't have one, and don't have it fully funded, you can't afford to pay towards college out of pocket.

Your retirement savings

Not saving for retirement? Aren't on track with your saving? Yep, you guessed it, you can't afford to help pay for college out of pocket. You should be using your cash to save for retirement first. There's a saying that "you can borrow for college, but not for retirement." I appreciate the sentiment, but I think it reinforces the (sometimes bad) idea that borrowing for college makes sense, and is THE RIGHT CHOICE. We'll talk more about borrowing later.

For right now, assume that saving for retirement is the better choice for you than paying for your child's college. We will discuss later if it makes sense to suspend saving for retirement for a short period WHILE YOUR CHILD IS IN SCHOOL, but that's also for later. You don't even have that option if you haven't been saving in the first place.

Let's just get this out there right now that I don't think withdrawing from retirement accounts to pay for college is a good thing either. Reasonable people can disagree here. There are advisors who recommend saving for college in a "Roth" account where you have the flexibility to withdraw contributions later with no taxes and no penalties. I have no problems with saving into a Roth account. It's the withdrawing

17

to pay for college part I have trouble with. Please leave your tax-advantaged retirement accounts alone. They aren't considered in the financial aid formula, they're there to help you WAY further out in the future, and in some cases, you'll be paying taxes and penalties to access that money.

Your other financial goals

Most people don't have unlimited money to cover everything they want. There are trade-offs you are going to have to make. It's ok to prioritize family vacations, paying down debt, children's current activities or other goals. Go back to your college money philosophy answers. What were you willing to do or give up? Add up the financial impact of all of that and write down that number for later if it means you'll have more money to pay for college.

Your outstanding debt

Do you have debt above and beyond a mortgage and a car loan? If you have credit card, medical, or student loan debt already, you can't afford to help pay for college. It just doesn't make sense. Your priority beyond digging that 5 bucks out of your couch to start your emergency fund should be getting out of debt.

Adding to your debt and expenses by borrowing more to send your child to college is going to get you in trouble financially. It's better to be honest with yourself right now before you go any further.

Your credit history and score

For the most part, new college students have no credit history and score, and so their individual borrowing options are limited. If you as a parent have a strong credit history and high credit score, you may have options for borrowing that make a lot of sense compared to others.

If you have a bankruptcy or other negative credit history, you might not even be able to take out parent loans or co-sign for your child. Not to say any of these options are the right thing to do, but it's important to know this now so you're not surprised later.

We'll talk all about borrowing to pay for school later, and the pros and cons of all the options.

Paying out of pocket

So, after going through all that, you should have a good handle on whether you can pay out of pocket and how much you can afford. It might not seem like much, but even if you can free up $100-$200 per month, that adds up to thousands of dollars you can contribute over time.

College specific savings/investing accounts

There's another chapter all about saving for college, but for many of you, that ship has sailed. You've either got college savings, or you don't. Figure out how much you have (and don't forget accounts grandparents might have set up!). Understand what kind of account it is, who owns it, how it is invested/what it earns, the rules for using the funds, and any tax benefits.

A lot of parents save in UTMA/UGMA (custodial) accounts. You need to understand that when your child reaches the age of majority in your state (usually 18 or 21), it's THEIR account. They don't have to use it for college. They don't have to use it responsibly. It's probably not a good idea to hide it from them, or drain it either. Trust me, I've seen it.

Other non-retirement resources

Some other resources I've seen families use for college are trusts and regular taxable investment accounts. Trusts are a tricky resource to understand. I will talk more about them in the financial aid chapter, but you might want to understand any trust you or your child is a beneficiary of, and whether anyone is entitled to distributions and when.

Taxable investment accounts in your own name (or under the name of a trust that you are the trustee of) are considered in the financial aid process as parental assets so you need to know how much is there.

Finally, did you buy beanie babies or baseball cards twenty years ago in hopes they would help pay for your child's college? Better check out how much they're worth today, and think about turning them – or any other stuff you have around the house – into cash before it's too late!

Your tax situation

It's important to understand that your tax filing status, marital status, state of residency, and income level all can impact whether your family can take advantage of some tax strategies. The government incentivizes taxpayers to contribute to higher education by offering credits and deductions. IRS Publication 970 – Tax Benefits for Higher Education spells it all out, but you're likely going to want to review everything with your tax preparer before and during this whole process. I don't plan to go through all of them in detail (income phase outs and availability can change year over year, and I'm not giving any tax advice here).

Here's what you need to know: to get some education tax benefits, you must be the parent taking the exemption for the student (regardless of who is paying the college expenses).

The three main tax strategies are:
- **American Opportunity Credit**
- **Lifetime Learning Credit**
- **Student Loan Interest Deduction**

The tricky thing about tax strategies is coordinating the expenses paid out of pocket/claimed on your taxes with any expenses you are paying out of tax-advantaged savings accounts. You can't double dip and use the same expenses more than once. They either count toward the tax credits/deductions OR may be considered "qualified" withdrawals from education savings accounts (Coverdell ESAs or 529 plans).

If you are a small business owner, there may be other strategies you can use to reduce your own personal income from the business, shift income from you to your child to take advantage of their lower tax bracket, or hold assets in a business account rather than a personal account. Depending on how the school you are looking at calculates financial aid, these strategies may or may not make a difference in the financial aid you receive. However, regardless of the effect on financial aid, they need to be weighed against the effect on your personal tax and financial situation.

The other thing about tax strategies is that they don't neces-sarily give you more money in your pocket in the year you are paying the bill for school (unless you are planning ahead). Pay attention to the lag in realizing the benefit of these strategies when you're putting together your college payment plan. You may have to wait for a tax refund next year.

Grandparent (or other) assistance

You may be lucky enough that your child's grandparents started a college savings account for them, or have offered to help pay for college. The grandparents have a whole set of financial considerations of their own to evaluate that are similar to yours. Their contributions can have consequences in areas like income, gift, and estate taxes. They should seek professional assistance when navigating these situations and do what's best for them.

However, I've seen parents who don't want to have this money conversation with their parents. They are embarrassed to ask for help or ask for details. Don't let that be you. You will need to understand from them how much they plan to contribute and when. You will need to share with them your current financial situation. You will need to share your financial aid results with them so that they don't affect any aid you receive going forward.

Planning for multiple children

Parents with multiple children have an especially daunting task. I recommend you lay out year by year which child is going to be in what grade, understand in which years there will be multiple children in college, understand your own ages and income each year, and understand which income years will be base years for financial aid (the income year that's counted in the freshman year financial aid offers for each child). You also need to realistically assess each child's strengths and weaknesses academically.

4

How Much Does College Cost?

Collge costs a lot more than when you went to school. In the last 20 years, the consumer price index has risen 51 percent according to the U.S. Bureau of Labor Statistics. Depending on which schools you're looking at, expect tuition, fees, and room and board to have increased around 250% - 300%, in comparison. After inflation, that's a 150%-175% increase. Average total cost of attendance is now about $48,500 per year for Private, non-profit, 4-year schools, and $21,000 per year for 4-year, in-state, at public schools.

Is an education worth more than it was 20 years ago? Schools want you to think so, but that's a topic for another chapter. Stay tuned.

The good news is that the rate of increase has been going down and was basically zero between the 2017-2018 and 2018-2019 school years. Colleges are finally seeing pushback, and smart parents have had enough. You're going to be one of those parents when you finish this book!

Why the large increases?

There is a lot that has gone into these increases.
- *Demand has increased.* Instead of being looked at a luxury for only the elite, going to college has become almost a requirement for many jobs and careers. It's the expectation for most high school students today.
- *Schools have been focused on attracting students.* They've been building fancy dorms, and providing gyms, rock climbing walls, lazy rivers and other amenities that are more like a country club or resort than a college. Someone has to pay for all those amenities.
- *At the same time, schools are hiring more administrators and professors, and paying them more.* Public schools have gotten less and less funding.

Do people pay "sticker price"?

"Sticker price" is the price that schools advertise and goes into the averages I quoted above. It is called the total Cost of Attendance (COA). But for years, most people haven't been paying that price. Schools are competing for students that are attractive in the areas of academic achievement, special talents, or diversity of population. They are offering academic-based or need-based aid to fill their freshman classes with the kinds of students they want. In essence, they're offering "discounts".

However, don't expect much "discounting" from public schools and schools where your student is not a standout for some reason compared to others that are applying. Highly competitive academic schools don't offer much (if any) in merit scholarships because everyone who attends is academically talented.

We'll discuss financial aid, scholarships, and more including something called the "Net Price Calculator" in future chapters. For now, just think of the cost of college as kind of like the price of an airline ticket. No two students at a school are likely paying the same price. The school sets prices and tries to maximize revenue for all the seats in the freshman class. They want to provide just enough of a "discount" to make you choose their school, but want to make sure you're paying the maximum you are willing to pay to attend.

Understand tuition costs

When you're looking at schools, one question to ask them is how they calculate tuition prices.

Some schools charge by the credit hour, so if your student takes less credits per semester, you pay less. At these schools, you only pay for the credits you take, but you'll want to make sure you're not paying for credits you won't need.

Some schools charge by the semester for a range of what they consider "full-time" credits. You pay the same amount whether the class load is at the bottom of the range or the top. At these schools, it pays to try and maximize the number of credits your student takes each semester to get the best value. Also understand how many credits must be taken each semester to graduate in four years. It's likely that by only taking the lower range of hours, your student won't graduate on time and it will result in extra semesters of tuition cost.

Little known tip: Check out regional tuition exchanges. These are programs where schools in the same region of the country have banded together. If you qualify, you could attend a school out-of-state for a reduced tuition. The NASFAA (National Association of Financial Aid Administrators) website offers more information and links to each region's exchange programs.

This is where I want to touch on in-state versus out-of-state tuition. For private schools, there's no difference. Tuition is tuition. For public schools, there can be a significant difference. Some parents think they can send their child to a school in another state (or move to the state) and then at some point the child will be eligible for in-state tuition. The reality is that states and schools have different criteria to qualify for in-state tuition. It's best to research this ahead of time. Some states are easy to qualify for, others nearly impossible.

Understand room and board costs

Schools have room and board packages that vary by housing unit, meal plan, occupancy, etc. Reported room and board prices are averages so it makes sense to consider what option you might choose.

Also, think about whether the school requires students to live on campus in university sponsored housing, or whether students can live off campus. In some areas with a high cost of living, it's cheaper to live on campus. In other areas, living off campus can significantly decrease costs. Of course, the cheapest option of all may be for your child to live at home and commute. Don't discount that option to save money, even if it's only for a year or two.

ALL the fees

I've seen reports of some schools gaming the system, and instead of increasing tuition, they add or increase fees. Regardless of what they call it, it's money you're paying to attend.

Typical (and some ridiculous-sounding) fees are:

- Orientation Fee
- Freshman Fee
- Campus Fee
- Commencement Fee
- Lab Fees
- Environment Fee
- Campus Spirit Fee
- Tech Fee
- Transportation Fee
- Athletic Fee

Other fees might be optional like student health fees, or fees for fraternities/sororities.

These fees will be listed out in your bill, but you should ask ahead of time which ones the school has, how much they are, and what they cover. Plan to utilize the services covered by the fee (like "free" shuttles covered by a transportation fee) to make the most of your money.

Although some of them might seem nominal, they can run into thousands of dollars in total. They may also vary by major or year in school. The bottom line is that they need to be in your budget and included in your total cost estimates.

Estimate books and supplies needed

This is still a huge cost that can run into the thousands per year. It will depend on major, year in school, and whether alternatives like electronic texts, used books, or borrowing books are options.

Estimate travel and transportation costs

If your child attends a school that is far away, trips home for breaks, holidays, and just getting there and back each semester can run into the thousands. Also plan for family travel for on campus visits, graduation, etc.

Another item to consider is whether the school allows students to have cars on campus. If so, you'll likely need to bake costs for car maintenance, gas, parking permits, and insurance into your (or your child's) budget. It may offset some of the travel costs, but may end up being more expensive once everything is added up.

Is extra equipment and decorating necessary?

I love all the questions I see every summer about dorm registries at Bed Bath and Beyond and which laptop is the best for college. Bottom line is that initial equipment for freshman year can run into the thousands so it's something you need to plan for in estimating your costs. The registry is a brilliant idea. See if you can get family and friends to help pay for some of this stuff.

On the other hand, I also have seen pictures and heard stories of dorm rooms that have been professionally designed and have all the latest technology. I mean, come on, really? Is this necessary? Your kid's room doesn't need its own Alexa, with coordinating curtains, rugs and bedding. Look into what the common areas provide and don't go crazy with this stuff. Buy used, or wait to buy entirely until your child gets to school and sees what they will really need.

Add it all up

If you see a theme here, it's that I'm asking you to WRITE IT DOWN (or put it in a spreadsheet). It's important to tally it all up and get the ugly total NOW, before you commit to a school and run out of cash before your child moves in.

5

Having "The Talk" With Your Child

I t's here where I ask you if you've talked about your College Money Philosophy, your College Money Reality, and the Cost of College with your child yet?

Money is an uncomfortable thing to talk about. In fact, many parents would prefer to talk about SEX with their kids rather than MONEY! This is because you may feel embarrassed about your financial situation. Maybe you haven't saved enough and wish you had started saving earlier. Maybe you don't talk about your expenses and your standard of living. You are NOT alone.

It's going to be awfully difficult to take the crazy out of the college admissions process if you haven't talked about your family finances with your child prior to going into it. They've probably already started talking about college with their friends. Maybe their friends have older siblings who have gone away to school. Does your child know where you went to school? Some families I've worked with have almost brought their children up to expect that they should attend their parents' alma mater. What if you can't afford that now that you're here?

Schedule time to have the "College Money Talk"

If you don't put it on the calendar, it won't happen. And no, don't wait until senior year of high school when your child is starting applications and you're getting ready to fill out the financial aid forms. Start talking with your child when they start high school, when they start talking about college options, or before. It's never too early.

Look at your College Money Reality with your child

Sit down and share results of your financial review exercise and college money philosophy exercise that you completed at the beginning of the book. Don't be embarrassed or apologetic. If you made financial mistakes in the past, share them so that your child might learn.

They should know the following:

- How much have you saved and will save going forward
- How much will you be able to pay out of pocket and if you plan to give them spending money
- How much do you expect your student to be responsible for – set expectations around whether they should plan to work to help save and pay for school, whether you expect them to contribute by taking out loans (and what that means to pay it back after they graduate), and whether you expect them to get scholarships
- The college budget – create a shopping budget and let your child know the consequences if you don't stick to it

Find out how your child feels about attending a school close to home to save money, or starting at a community college and then transferring. Find out how certain they are about major, school size preferences, and what kind of experience they want out of college. Although it's hard to recognize, your child is becoming a young adult. It's important for them to understand and be involved in the college money decisions.

6

Saving for College

I f your child is already in high school, and you haven't already saved for college, you have permission to skim this chapter. Not to say that you can't still save, but it just isn't as impactful as it could have been. The whole point of saving is to take advantage of compounding interest and investment returns over time, along with tax benefits for some savings options.

For those of you who have more slack in your timeline, go back to the College Money Reality chapter to make sure you've covered all your other bases before you direct money toward saving for college.

If you already have savings that are earmarked for college, pay special attention to how the account can be used. There are usually rules on how college savings accounts can be used to maximize their benefits. You don't want to run afoul of any legal or tax rules.

How much should I save toward college?

So now that you're ready to put money aside – there are a couple of questions you likely have. What kind of account should you use, and how much should you save?

I'm going to get the "how much" question out of the way first. That's because the answer is a total guess on anyone's part, including mine. If you've ever used a retirement calculator, you punch in all the numbers and out pops a completely ridiculous estimate of what you should be saving monthly to retire at a certain age.

College savings calculators are even worse for a couple of reasons. The timeframe is usually relatively short compared to retirement. This affects how long any earnings can compound, as well as how risky you might feel comfortable being with any investment.

The other problem is that many calculators "bake in" a high increase in the cost of attendance to the calculation and come up with an estimate of more than $100,000 PER YEAR in the future. The savings recommendation that comes out of this can be something ridiculous like $2000 per month per child for the next 10 years. I'm sure you have this money sitting around just wondering what to do with it.

Nobody can predict what the future will bring as to the price of a higher education, or what your savings might earn over time. I ask clients to go through the college money philosophy exercise and evaluate their finances, and then decide how much they CAN and WANT to save. Every dollar you can save is a dollar you won't have to count on coming from somewhere else while your child is in school.

It's not likely you can save the entire cost of paying for college before your child reaches 18 anyway. You will need a variety of resources to cover it all. Some can come from savings, some will come out of cash flow, some can come from your child working, some from loans and scholarships, and some from family. A good ballpark is to try and save enough in order to pay about 1/3 the cost of college out of savings.

What is the "right" account to use to save for college?

Here's where I tell you that there isn't a general right answer. If I knew everything about you, and your family's financial situation, I could recommend a few options that would be a better fit than others. But since I don't, I'm going to let you know what some options are, and some information about each. It's going to be up to you to decide which one is best for you.

Don't buy life insurance to save for college

There is however, one way of "saving" I tell everyone to avoid. Do not buy a "life insurance" policy that builds "cash value" that you can "borrow against" to pay for school. This is not a good way to save for college. I will talk about this more in the chapter about who you can trust, but take my word for it right now that you shouldn't do it. Life insurance is not savings.

Criteria to decide which type of savings is best

There are several criteria that can help you decide which option is best for you.

Tax benefits – One reason people save for college is because of the federal income tax, gift tax, estate tax, and/or state tax benefits from doing so. Based on your personal tax situation, those benefits may apply to you or not.

How much you can save – Some accounts have maximums on how much you can contribute yearly.

Qualified expenses – what expenses tied to college qualify to be able to take advantage of the tax benefit?

Ability to change the beneficiary – can you change the beneficiary of the account in case the original one does not attend?

Age/time restrictions – are there any age or time restrictions for contributions, withdrawals, or tax benefits?

Income restrictions – can you contribute based on income?

Financial aid impact – where does this money fit in the financial aid formula as it sits in the account, and then when it is withdrawn?

Investments – what kind of investments are allowed in this kind of account?

And finally, what happens if you use the account for something other than educational purposes?

Section 529 savings plans

I want to give special detail about Section 529 savings plans because of how popular they have become. Don't believe people who tell you this is a bad way to save for college. Like all options, they have good and bad points. Don't confuse savings plans with Section 529 Pre-Paid Tuition Plans, those are a completely separate animal. If you have a Pre-Paid Tuition Plan, you'll want to understand the benefits and limitations of your specific plan.

Tax advantages – 529 plans were created back in the 90s to encourage people to save for college by creating tax advantages for doing so. Investments in 529 plans grow tax-free and all earnings in 529 plans can be withdrawn tax-free if the withdrawal is used for qualified education expenses. In addition, some states' plans give residents a tax break on the money you put into the plan in the form of a deduction to income. Some states even offer matching funds.

Ownership – Anyone can open and own a 529 plan. That makes it an option for grandparents, aunts, uncles, parents, or complete strangers to save for your child's education. You can also open a 529 plan for yourself, helpful if you plan to attend grad school down the road. The other option is a custodial 529 plan. You can often rollover funds from a UTMA/UGMA account into this kind of 529 and it may improve your financial aid situation.

Beneficiaries – There can be only one beneficiary per account, but the owner can change the beneficiary to another family member if the original one decides not to attend college or if there are funds left over.

Flexibility – Money in a 529 Savings Plan (not the pre-paid tuition variety) can be used at almost any accredited college in the country, and some international ones eligible for Federal Financial Aid. You can also use the money for many different expenses besides tuition, like room & board, fees, books and supplies.

Funding – Many plans allow you to set up regular contributions and have low minimum opening requirements. You can also front-load contributions up to 5 years times the annual federal gift tax exclusion in one year. This gives your money more time to grow.

Fees – as with any investment, there are fees associated that can vary widely depending on the plan you are looking at. It seems like everyone takes their cut on many 529 options. There are account maintenance fees, asset fees, state fees, and manager fees.

Limited investments – many plans have a mix of options from age-based portfolios to investments with guaranteed returns. Your options are limited by the plan, however, and you can only change your investment choice twice a year. It's important to understand your risk tolerance and time horizon because your investment could lose money and you don't want to come up short if the market dives right before your child goes off to school.

Penalties – If your original beneficiary doesn't use the money for qualified education expenses, and you can't/don't designate a new beneficiary, then your earnings are subject to a 10% penalty when you withdraw them. Contributions can always be withdrawn without penalty, but most 529 plans pro-rate withdrawals between contributions and earnings so at least some portion of a withdrawal may be taxed and penalized.

Direct-sold v. Advisor-sold – Many states' plans give you the option of going directly to a website to open a 529 account (or calling a phone number, or filling out a paper application), or you can choose to go to a financial advisor. The reason this is so ugly is that going through the advisor can cost you thousands of dollars more than going direct. The idea is that the advisor will give you good advice if you need it, but there have been cases of advisors recommending out of state plans instead of their own state's (tax advantaged) plans just to earn higher commissions. The advisors may also be limited in the plans they can recommend depending on who they are working for. If you need advice, you are much better served going to a fee-only or hourly financial planner who will give you unbiased advice and help you enroll in the direct option that is best for you.

Treatment in financial aid - Funds in these plans are treated as a parent asset if owned by the child (custodial account) OR the parent (even if the beneficiary is a sibling). Withdrawals if owned by parent or child are ignored in financial aid unless for some reason they are not qualified and are taxable income. Funds in grandparent-owned accounts (or ones owned by anyone else), are not assets for financial aid. Funds are considered untaxed income/support of the student, and will be tied to the year of the withdrawal.

Other savings options

Some other popular savings options are:

Coverdell education savings accounts (ESA)

Contributions to these accounts are non-deductible for Federal Income Tax. Earnings can be exempt from tax if used for qualified higher education expenses (or K-12). The maximum that can be contributed is $2,000 per beneficiary, per year, in total. You can change the beneficiary much like the 529 accounts. There are restrictions on the age limit for contributions (age 18) and use of the account (age 30) that are more restrictive than the 529. There are also income restrictions on those who can contribute. Their treatment in the financial aid process is similar to the 529 account.

U.S. savings bonds

Purchase of qualifying U.S. Savings Bonds are tax-deferred for federal; tax-free for state; and certain post-1989 EE and I bonds may be redeemed federal tax-free for qualified higher education expenses. There are caps on the maximum investment you can make per year, per owner, and per type of bond. The qualified expenses that these can be used for are more narrow than 529 and ESA accounts. There are age and income restrictions for the bond purchaser/owner and they are counted as assets of the owner/parent in the financial aid formula.

UGMA/UTMA (custodial) accounts

Contributions made to these accounts are gifts to the minor owner of the account. The earnings of the account are taxed to the minor with a small exclusion that is tax exempt. The benefit of these accounts is there are no maximum investments, and no income/age restrictions for contributions. The drawback as I mentioned earlier is that the account becomes available to your child at the age of majority in your state. The other downside is the account is counted as a student asset in financial aid. You'll learn later why this is important. One option is to convert this type of account into a custodial 529 account as I mentioned above so that it will be counted under the parent asset type for financial aid. This can make a significant difference in financial aid eligibility depending on the size of the account, and the rest of your financial picture.

Google "comparison of college savings options" to get more information.

7

Who Should You Trust?

Today it's easier than ever to find answers to your questions. But how do you know if it's the right answer? Is there a right answer? There might be just one or two versions of an answer that are right for you.

In the college admissions process, there are a lot of people involved and the stakes are high. You're likely to be seeking answers from at least one or more of the following:

- Friends and Family
- High School Counselor
- College Administrators
- College Consultants
- CPA
- Financial Advisor
- Facebook/Online Groups
- Google

Instead of telling you exactly who you should trust, I'm going to give you some criteria on how to think about this challenge with each group. I will say off the top that it's possible to get wrong answers and bad advice from anywhere and anyone. Usually, people do the best to give the right answer and help you out, but it doesn't hurt to think critically when evaluating their advice.

Friends and family

Let's start with friends and family. As soon as you start talking about college with them, the advice probably comes faster than you can digest it. They like to give advice on which schools your child should apply to, boast about how their kid got a "full ride at X school", and complain how they got screwed by the financial aid system. They're going to have opinions about loans, school location, dorms, and what others would think if your child did X, Y, or Z after high school. Just like you, they are emotionally invested in this decision.

When dealing with friends and family, I encourage you to take it all in, but with a grain of salt. Develop your own response to these conversations like "Thank you for that advice" or "That's interesting" that will shut it down if you want. Or, you could ask a few questions and decide how deep you want to go in the conversation. It can be like discussing politics at the dinner table – tread carefully.

Some people are going to take it personally if your child doesn't apply to the school they recommended. Others will ask probing questions about your finances, or even lie about the financial aid/scholarships they received. I swear this happens.

When the noise gets to be too much, go back to your College Money Philosophy stuck to your refrigerator or bathroom mirror. Remember your own beliefs and priorities.

High school counselor

This person is an important piece of the puzzle when it comes to college. They are there to help your children make smart academic and extracurricular decisions that will support their future success. Their advice can be invaluable when you want to make sure your child is tracking to graduate on time with a transcript that's attractive to the colleges they are interested in.

It's unfortunate that many high school counselors have large numbers of students they support. Your child may not be able to get in to see them as often as they need, and may not develop as close of a relationship as they would like to. Make the most of the time you have with them. They are key during the college admissions process with advice about schools, application requirements, recommendations, and transcripts.

There are a few areas where I would advise extra consideration. Counselors may be comfortable and knowledgeable about only a subset of schools, and ones they work with often. It's impossible for them to know everything about the thousands of 4-yr and 2-yr schools that are out there. Remember that high schools boast about which colleges their seniors are planning to attend. Do your own research and add other schools to any list that your child works on with their counselor.

The other area to tread lightly on is the financial aid process. This is the area I want you to think most critically about. Counselors often don't know much about your family finances and aren't experts in financial aid. The school suggestions they provide are likely to include some that are not a financial fit for your family and that you could not afford to attend. However, they may have great information on local scholarships your child may be eligible for based on their profile.

Every high school has a "financial aid night". The information provided during these presentations ranges from basic and helpful to useless and harmful. It's important to consider who is giving the presentation, what their credentials and experience are, and what their motive is. After being burned by so-called "financial advisors" using this opportunity as only a sales pitch, schools either use their own staff to present, or partner with a local college financial aid administrator. Expect to get some good information, but don't count on this short presentation to get all your financial aid questions answered.

College administrators

College administrators can help you the most when they are answering your questions about their school, their processes, and their criteria. They are the ones to go to for admissions questions, and financial aid questions specific to their school: such as timeline and school scholarships. They will guide you to resources on the school's website where you can find answers to your questions.

Be careful when asking for advice on your own personal situation. Around finances, they may have an incentive to help you figure out a way to attend their school, even if it's not affordable. They aren't going to know all the ins and outs of your personal financial situation. They are there to help the school fill the freshman class with desirable students. This is not to say their advice isn't valid, just make sure you step back and think about yourself first.

College consultants

This is an area that's exploded in popularity recently. I know and have worked with several consultants in my practice who can't keep up with all the new business they are generating. I think this speaks to how scared and unprepared so many parents feel to face this journey alone. They want someone who can help guide them.

I think college consultants can be invaluable in a couple of areas: college fit/admissions assistance, and test preparation. Some do both, some only do one or the other. Think about your budget and what your family could benefit from the most. Subsequent chapters will focus on how important both areas are from a financial perspective but here I will give you an overview of how consultants work.

Ones who focus on college fit/admissions are working with you to help your child find the best possible social and academic fit. They want to get to know your child and help them build a college list that works with their interests and strengths. They may help with admissions timelines, essays, and cracking the whip so you don't have to do it. Your child may be much more likely to listen to a neutral third party who encourages rather than nags. That alone could be worth the fee!

The best consultants have packages available to fit a variety of budgets and needs. They have experience either in college admissions roles or school counselor roles. I would say to steer clear of any who promise that working with them will guarantee admittance to top tier schools, and boast about all the fancy schools their clients have been admitted to. Again, if it's too good to be true, it can get you in trouble with the law down the road! (Google college admissions scandals or financial aid scandals if you don't know what I mean)

The other kind of consultant I like is the one who focuses on helping your child prepare for, and improve, their SAT or ACT test scores. Most students should take these tests more than once to get the highest score possible – because higher scores can cut what you pay for college dramatically! Consultants in this area work with students in a variety of ways to help them improve.

Who you should pick to help with test scores depends on the needs of your child. Some will focus more on test-taking strategies to help students become familiar with the types of questions asked. Some will focus on improving knowledge in academic/knowledge areas your child tests poorly on during practice tests. Still others will focus on psychological strategies if your child struggles with anxiety around test-taking and being under the clock.

The best ones have experience as teachers, tutors, or psychologists. They usually work hourly with students one-on-one, have packages available, or hold group classroom sessions. The important part is knowing what your child would benefit from. If your child is the type that can be self-motivated, they could hop online and get free help from a variety of online resources like Khan Academy. If they work well in a group setting, a classroom might be the right fit. If they need more personalized attention, one-on-one coaching could work best. Again, a neutral third party to crack the whip may be well worth it!

CPA or tax preparer

Your CPA is a great resource for you to ask questions about tax deductions and credits for education related expenses/student loan interest. They should also be familiar with the rules surrounding coordination of withdrawals from various college savings accounts with money paid out of pocket, and help you make sure you are following the IRS rules.

Another area they may be able to help in is understanding your income tax return and how various components are used in the financial aid formulas. They could help you plan for the future by suggesting ways you could optimize your return to gain more financial aid.

But be careful. I've seen situations where tax advice that is solid for tax purposes can instead negatively impact the overall financial picture of the family. I have also seen where CPAs who are unfamiliar with education situations and financial aid give incorrect advice that could subject your family to reduced financial aid or get you caught in an audit.

Consider looking for a CPA who has experience in these areas, but at the same time isn't trying to upsell you on services you may not need. Taxes in general are an area where I think many families just stick their heads in the sand and don't pay close attention to what their CPA is doing. Ask questions and ask for explanations in plain English until you can understand what strategies they are recommending and why. If something sounds too good to be true, it usually is.

Financial advisor

Ahhh. The financial advisor. Since I am one, it's tricky for me to claim unbiased opinions here. But I'm going to anyway. One of the reasons I became a financial planner was because of all the bad/conflicted advice people get from those already in the industry. As I mentioned before, I'm a fiduciary and I'm legally bound to give advice in the best interests of my clients. Most who call themselves "advisors" are NOT.

There are two types of situations I want to describe here. You should think carefully about what I'm saying.

If your family already has a financial advisor, think about the kind of advice they give you today. Are they making recommendations around your family's comprehensive financial situation? Are they just managing your investment accounts? Are they mainly an insurance agent or investment broker?

There are so many kinds of people that are covered under the broad "financial advisor" title. It's important to consider how they are compensated and think about how that incentivizes them to answer your questions and help your family through the college admissions process. If they earn more by recommending insurance or investment products, it's likely their advice will center around those solutions. If they earn more by managing your investments, their advice may focus on investment-related decisions.

It's not that their advice is WRONG, per se. It's just not the BEST advice for your family, in many cases. They are conflicted by their relationship to the company where they work, or the compensation they can earn on the products they sell. Ask them if they have specific experience helping families with kids going to college, and listen carefully to their answers about how they

49

can help you during this time. Again, if it seems too good to be true, it probably is.

If your current advisor isn't the right one to help you, there's nothing wrong with looking for a specialist in this area. When your child enters high school, you're going to start receiving all kinds of mail, emails, facebook ads, etc from people claiming they know how your family can beat the financial aid system and pay less to go to college. These advertisements usually focus on "loopholes" in the system and "secrets" only this person knows.

While there are some strategies that families can use (and this book contains everything I know of), if you've watched the news lately, some of those strategies can get you into trouble with the law or school later. Even if they are technically "legal".

Again, they also might not be the best choice for your family's finances overall, and may not even work because the person selling the strategy doesn't know your complete situation. They have a hammer, and to them everything looks like a nail. Unfortunately for you, you often have to pay out of pocket first before you learn that their strategy doesn't work for you. I've heard of intimidation and scare tactics some of these "advisors" use that make me sick.

The reality is that there are very few advisors like me. Ones who aren't selling any products related to secrets and loopholes, and who get paid a fee strictly for unbiased advice. There are even fewer of us who have the expertise on the college financial journey. But we are out there. Start with www.crazycollege-money.com. We can also be found on the NAPFA or XY Planning Network website when you search for specialties in college planning and student loans.

Facebook/online groups

Social media sites like Facebook have made it easy to connect with others in your similar situation and share information. I'm a part of a bunch of Facebook groups for parents with college bound children, groups that help you figure out how to pay for college, and I'm even an admin of one where you can ask questions of experts in this field of college financial advice. There is some great information to be found in these groups. Crazy College Money has its own Facebook group as well.

However, I have seen a few problems. Some of the advice and answers people receive are just plain wrong. Either the responder didn't understand the question, they aren't applying the rules correctly, or they think that just because something worked for them, it will work for someone else. Be careful sharing too many details of your personal financial situation in a public forum like this.

Some people join or start these groups so they can sell their system, their product, or their service. There isn't anything inherently wrong with this; you just need to know who the person is and what their motivations are. Some admins are very clear about the purpose of the group. Some members give helpful advice in addition to suggesting something where they benefit from it.

The other problem is that if you think friends and family are bad at judging you and making drama, online it's even worse. There are people out there with nothing better to do than shame you, troll you, opine about your situation or your question, and generally make online life miserable. Admins usually try their best to weed these people out, but they can slip through the cracks. Take it all with a grain of salt and leave the group if you don't feel comfortable.

Google

You might be surprised to know that I google almost every question I get from others or have myself – and I've already told you to Google a bunch of them in this book. I generally believe that the right answer is out there, I just need to find it.

There are a couple of ways Googling something can be really helpful: this is where you can find great primary resources like the federal student student aid website, the IRS publication that deals with education topics, or helpful college search websites. You don't have to remember all of this yourself.

The other way Google is helpful is in showing you mainstream media sources that have written articles that answer your question. Sources like Forbes, the Wall Street Journal, and other newspapers and television channels all publish articles/videos on important topics surrounding paying for college. Often, they provide better information than the random person on the Facebook group.

There's also a lot of junk out there. I'm a professional so I know how to separate the junk from the good stuff. I know which sources reliably provide accurate answers and which to ignore. You may not be able to do that at first, but you'll get better at it the more you do it. The other option is to start following me and others like myself on Twitter, Facebook, LinkedIn and reading our blogs, as well as listening to our podcasts. Our goal is to separate the good information from the bad and cut down some of the noise. There are also chapter by chapter resources at www.crazycollegemoney.com that you can reference which will show the best results of the google searches I mention throughout the book.

8

The Postcard Budget

Here's where the rubber meets the road and you're going to start figuring out how much you're going to contribute to pay for college. Remember there's no Financial Aid Fairy. Regardless of how little money you make or have, schools are going to expect you to pay something toward college. You need to figure out your budget first.

I'm a big fan of keeping things simple. Get out a postcard (or spreadsheet) for each school your child is interested in/plans to apply to. You're going to be filling in the dollar amounts as you go through the process, but here's where you should be so far. Leave the dollar amounts on the first 4 lines blank for now. Fill in dollar amounts (even if they are $0) where the gray boxes are, leaving Student Work Study and Federal Direct Student Loan blank.

School A – Year One		
Total Cost of Attendance	$	
Subtract Grants (Free-Money)	$	
Subtract Scholarships (Semi-Free Money)	$	
Equals		
Amount Your Family Has to Cover	$	
Savings Withdrawal	$	5,000
Tax Savings	$	500
Parent Cash Flow ($1,000/month)	$	12,000
Student Summer Job	$	2,000
Student Work Study	$	
Grandparents/Other	$	1,000
Federal Direct Student Loan	$	
Total Budget	$	20,500

Add up the numbers you just wrote down. This is your budget. In the example above, your budget is $20,500 per year. Did I mention you need to have a budget, FIRST? Do not go visit schools, fill out applications, or apply for financial aid before you know your budget.

9

There ARE Colleges You Can't Afford

Here we are. Now, you know your budget. After assessing your finances and calculating how much you can contribute, you must face the truth. There are colleges you can't afford. Say it again to yourself. There are schools we can't afford to send our child to. Now take a deep breath.

It's not comfortable. It's not popular in our consumer-driven society to say we can't afford something. Your child may be disappointed. You'll have the college money talk and they may not talk to you for a while because they're angry. That's life. Better to learn it now before somebody gets into a pile of debt they can't pay back. You're going to be one of those families where reality rules.

Does the reality of the situation match your College Money Philosophy? Or do you need to reconsider how you think about paying for school? Are there other ways you can contribute such as letting your child live at home?

If there is some wiggle room in your finances, I recommend dividing schools up into three categories: No way, Maybe, and

Budget-Friendly (financial safety). The "Maybe" schools can stay on the list a while longer until you assess the financial aid situation at that school. Adding in the amounts for Student Work Study and Federal Direct Student Loans in the budget worksheet may bump a school into the Maybe category.

I'm not going to belabor this point (except for a little). We can't afford XYZ University. ABC College is not in our budget. The first time you say it, it's hard. It will get easier. You will feel more confidence each time. Secretly, your friends and family will be impressed. Don't expect anyone to pat you on the back, though. It's human nature for misery to want company. You're going to disappoint everyone who wants you to buy into the hype and be miserable paying for a college you can't afford.

10

Is College (Still) a Good Investment?

When you look at your budget, you may start thinking that it sure would be nice to spend that money on something like a nice vacation. You may start asking yourself if college is really a good investment. I don't like this question for a couple of reasons. I will still answer it, but let me explain why I don't like it.

First, using the word "investment" implies that the parent is the investor and they are expecting some kind of return on that investment. If anyone is the investor, it's the student. They are investing time and maybe some money in the hopes that they get a better paying job in the future or some other benefit from having a college degree.

As a parent "investor", you have no control over the outcome and the benefit of the investment is not coming your way in the future. You can argue that it will. Maybe your kids won't be living in your house forever if they get a good job. Maybe they will help support you in your old age because they can afford it then. You are not required to let them live in your house, and I will argue that you need to be able to take care of yourself first by planning for your retirement rather than paying for college.

Second, it's backward looking. Studies that show the "value of a college degree" are tracking previous college graduates in total and comparing their earnings over time to those who didn't go to college. They have nothing to do with what the future will look like for future college graduates. If you know anything about "investing", you know that past performance does not guarantee future results.

College graduates of the past had a completely different set of circumstances they have lived through. The economy, the job market, the technology, and the world have all changed. There are more college graduates than ever before, so it's not the leg up it used to be. What made some people successful in the past may not be what makes them able to earn more money in the future.

Third, it's too broad. There are many ways to be successful and earn money. Some may attend college and gain skills and knowledge that an employer values. They go on to get a great job, have a successful career, and feel like going to college was a "good investment". Others may slide through college just to check the degree box, not be able to find a well-paying job when they graduate because they don't have anything to offer an employer, and blame college as a "bad investment". Some others didn't go to college, but instead got a certification or did an apprenticeship, started a business, and became very successful – maybe even more than the first group. Did this have anything to do with the fact that they didn't go to college?

So is college still a good idea? In a word, yes. Those who are smart about how much they spend/borrow, what school they go to, what they major in, and what they do in life after they graduate do benefit from higher education. Those who aren't, don't.

A word about graduate school

As more and more undergraduate degrees have been awarded, some jobs/careers are requiring additional degrees to make applicants stand out, or even as a prerequisite. I advocate thinking very critically about how much you want to spend on an undergraduate degree for your child in a field where a graduate degree is required.

In addition, people are spending and borrowing ridiculous amounts of money to get graduate degrees that don't pay off in the long run too (including my MBA). There are tons of horror stories about MBAs, lawyers, and doctors who have borrowed hundreds of thousands of dollars and then can't pay their loans. But that's a topic for another book.

All that being said, I think that, in general, our society still rewards those who gain skills and knowledge that enable them to go out into the job world and add value for an employer. Going to college and getting a degree is not a guarantee of anything. It's up to your child to make the most of the opportunity.

Again on planning for multiple children

This book is really focused on planning for one child, usually your oldest because that's when you don't know anything going into it. For those of you with more than one child, your life is a little more complicated. Instead of a 4-6 year process, college planning can be a 10-15 year process. Having multiple children means it's even more important to go through the process for the oldest with the long term in mind. Write out the timing of when each child will be in high school and college. Find out when you will have multiple children in college. Look at how old you will be when the youngest is finished and compare that to when you want to retire.

Each one of your children will have different strengths and interests. The college search will vary for each of them and your financial picture will change over time. Your oldest may be more academically talented and receive more scholarships. You may have higher income when the youngest goes to college and may be able to pay more out of pocket. The key is to think about this timeline when your oldest starts high school. There will be options, such as borrowing large amounts to send the oldest to their dream school, that will be less of a good idea if there are younger children to follow.

11

School Matters

P eople go crazy about rankings. I'm here to tell you that they generally don't matter. If you consider some of the criteria that goes into most rankings, you might agree. Even if you don't agree with me, media rankings should not be your starting point in creating a college list with your child.

There are reasonable ranking inputs like graduation and retention rates that are included in the most popular lists. But just as important, there should be measures like percentage of graduates that have a job upon graduation. As well as how much are they earning in their field. After all, you want to know if your student will graduate on time and get a job that can pay the bills.

Stupid criteria, in my opinion, are ones like "expert opinion", "school selectivity" and "alumni giving". Who cares what others in the same educational industry bubble think about each other's institutions? Does admitting a small number of applicants matter? How do alumni donations have anything to do with how successful your child will be at that school and in life? It seems to me like there is a whole lot of fluff in these rankings.

If you're going to look at rankings, make sure you understand what goes into them, and decide if those criteria matter to you. Instead of putting your faith in media rankings, decide what criteria matter to your family. I would advocate that you should be looking at a few that are truly important.

Graduation rate

You will be amazed, when you start researching colleges, at how dismal these rates are. Average four-year graduation rates are around 33% for public schools and 53% for private schools. Four-year graduation rates are so bad at so many schools, they focus on reporting SIX-year graduation rates. The "Student Right to Know" graduation rate is the six-year graduation rate. You should look more closely to find the four-year rate. I know that most people don't plan to pay for six years of college for their child. It's up to you to decide what a good 4-yr graduation rate is to you - at a minimum I recommend 40%.

Job placement statistics

This data is a little trickier to find. You may need to dig around, ask schools directly, or ask departments about graduates in specific majors. If you think getting a job is one outcome that is important, it's worth the time spent. It can be tough for schools to get this information from their graduates, and what they do report may not be accurate or include everyone. Consider the context of what is being reported.

75th Percentile test scores

Many people focus on average test scores because they are thinking about the likelihood of their child getting into the school. Instead, this metric will tell you a little about the likelihood of receiving merit (academic)-based financial aid from the school. If your student is in the top quarter of the incoming freshman class, they are much more likely to receive money from the school in the form of scholarships that are not based on financial need.

Other school statistics

Size

One of the first ways to cut down the list of potential schools is to focus on the size of the school. What many don't realize is that there are a LOT more smaller schools than larger schools. Many of the larger schools will be out of state public schools for you, which means their cost is going to be as high as a private school. Size will affect financial aid. The more flexible you can be on size, the more options you will have to receive generous aid packages that will lower your out of pocket cost to attend.

Class size/% taught by professors

Some students thrive in big classes, others do better with more individualized attention. Does your child want to be instructed by teaching assistants or professors, and do they want to be able to engage with their instructors outside the classroom?

School location

Start thinking about what type of setting your child likes – urban, rural, mountains, beach? Should school be close to home or across the country? There are definitely locations that are much more expensive than others to live in and travel to.

School matters, not ranking

The school certainly matters but not because of the ranking and the name on the sticker on the back of your car. Students, along with their parents, need to find the right academic and social fit for themselves. They will be happier at a good fit school, perform better, learn more, graduate on time, and get a job so they can move out of your house. The ranking of some media outlet doesn't matter when it comes down to your family's decision. As for financial fit and why school matters, we'll get to that shortly.

An aside about for-profit schools

I think it goes without saying that I am only referring to and thinking about not-for-profit colleges and universities in this book. At least I hope it does.

For-profit institutions have exploded in number over the last couple of decades. They can tap into federal funds for education, but often don't have the accreditation and educational rigor traditional not-for-profit schools have. They have been under scrutiny for misleading applicants about job placement statistics, saddling students and non-graduates with student loan debt, and generally not being worth their high cost. Some schools have shut down without warning and left their students high and dry. If you choose to look at for-profit schools, you should beware of these criticisms.

12

Major Matters

One of the first ways to narrow down the list of schools in consideration is to search by major. That's great for those who are certain what they want to study. However, if your child doesn't know what they want to major in, don't freak out. Over time, about a third of students switch majors. I switched from Biology to Spanish. Then went back to school for Computer Science. Here's what to think about now during this process and how it impacts the financial choices you're making.

Some majors lead to higher paying jobs

It's an unavoidable fact – engineering graduates earn way more than teachers. I don't mean to suggest that students pick a major based on how much money they can earn at graduation, but it needs to be a consideration. If your child can't decide, it doesn't hurt to think about the job market, and majors that are in demand by employers.

Major can drive school cost and admissions

At some schools, students can apply directly to undergraduate programs in areas like business, engineering, or music. These programs may be more competitive than others at the same school and decrease their chance for admission and financial aid. There also may be different costs depending on the major. It's important to understand this going in.

It might be harder to graduate on time

There are a couple of reasons this might be the case for your child. One, changing major may mean a whole new set of introductory courses that must be taken. These will have to be scheduled out over time and could push out the graduation timeline. Two, it may be more difficult to get into prerequisite classes for some majors because the numbers of students admitted to a major exceeds the spots available. This problem is called "impaction" and it's a huge reason students can't graduate on time at some state schools, especially in California where I live.

From a cost perspective, I think it makes sense to have a few majors in mind, be flexible in programs of study, and plan to take lower level classes that can qualify for several majors.

13

The College List

Now the hard part comes in starting to help your child come up with a list of schools. Schools can be separated out into categories based on selectivity, size, and public v. private. It would be great if these categories had clear delineations about how much financial aid they offer. And they do, kind of. But there is no clear winner, that's for sure. More on that later. Let's take a step back first.

What is "Net Price"?

I mentioned earlier that almost no one pays the "sticker price" to attend a school. Net Price is the price you actually pay after financial aid is factored in. This is the formula:

COA – Financial Aid = Net Price

We talked a little bit above about the total cost of attendance (COA) when we talked about how much college costs these days, and we'll talk below about Financial Aid. Right now, let's focus on Net Price.

What is the net price calculator?

In 2008, a mandate was passed by the Department of Education that required all schools who receive federal aid funds to include a calculator on their website that allows consumers to estimate what their out-of-pocket costs would be to attend that school. This is important because most people do not pay the "sticker price" posted on the school's website. Schools use a variety of need-based and merit-based financial aid to help them attract the students they want to have at their school. Financial aid is part of their secret sauce and they really didn't want to have to share that information with the public.

Fast-forward to 2019, and there are a variety of ways schools have chosen to implement this mandate. Some schools' calculators are better than others. Typically, the more information they ask for, the better estimate they give you. If they don't ask about grades or test scores, they won't be able to give you an estimate of academic financial aid using those factors.

Some of these calculators are just plain crappy. I've seen ones that are still using 2016 numbers in their current version. I'm sorry, people at NIU, I really don't care about costs in 2016-2017. How about an update?? The NIU calculator says that their estimate includes merit and need based aid, but how can it when it doesn't even ask about the grades and test scores of the student? I want to run through a few of the types of Net Price Calculators, and why it's important to you, the parent, and me, the financial advisor. I'll start first with the Federal Template.

The federal template

To make it easier for schools to comply with the 2008 mandate, the federal government developed a simple template that schools could hook into and post on their websites very easily. It's totally basic, and does little more than meet the requirement. In my opinion, it doesn't ask enough questions to really let you get a sense of what YOUR Net Price at that school will be, but at least it can give you an idea if you qualify for need-based aid in general.

You can tell schools that use this template because they typically have a really old "clip art" picture of a calculator on their Net Price Calculator page. In general, I think schools who use the federal template do a pretty awful job helping consumers out, but that's just one thing to keep in mind as you assess where you want to spend your hard-earned college tuition dollars. At least it's a step in the right direction for transparency.

Better net price calculators

For some schools, the mandate has given them the opportunity to really show what it might cost to attend their school. These schools have partnered with 3rd party calculator-creators to implement pretty robust estimates. There are multiple companies who offer this service to schools, and as you try out calculators of different schools, you will probably recognize several of them.

These calculators allow the student to get a better estimate, and the school to provide a better estimate. Better estimates benefit both parties.

What does a good calculator ask? It asks all the questions necessary to help determine your estimated EFC (Expected

Family Contribution) like student grade, geographical location, marital status, and dependency status. It also asks parent information on their marital status, ages, legal residence, siblings, and how many will be in college. It asks about student and parent assets and income too.

If the school uses their own Financial Aid formula, it may ask additional questions for more detail on parent and student assets, taxes, adjustments to income, medical expenses, private school tuition you're paying, and home equity.

Good calculators also ask about student GPA and standardized test scores (ACT and SAT), and I've even seen some that ask about National Merit Scholarship finalist status and other academic recognitions.

This might seem kind of creepy to you and you might not want to share this information. However, the more information you can share, and the more accurately you fill out the school's calculator, the better your Net Price estimate will be. If you're trying to express interest in a school and show them what a strong candidate you are, some even give you the chance to save your information (i.e. "Sign up for an account"). You need to weigh whether or not you want to do this.

The amazing part

As a financial planner, the amazing part is the insight these calculators give me (and you!) into the financial aid processes of the school. I typically feel like the ones who use the federal template are not very helpful. The ones who use better calculators allow consumers to do a little testing to see what may move the needle on financial aid.

Would a higher GPA or test score translate into more potential merit aid? Enter that information into the calculator and see what the output is. Does the school care about home equity? Enter various figures for home equity and see if it changes the estimates. What kinds of special circumstances do they care about? If I can strategize about income timing and asset placement with a family, what will that get them (if anything) in additional financial aid?

It's worth your time to spend a little time trying out the calculators of the schools your family is interested in. In no time, you'll be able to spot the good ones and understand more about the financial priorities and processes of those schools!

Financial aid generalizations

I'm going to throw out some broad categories of schools, and rules of thumb about their financial aid. But to start getting an idea of what you might qualify for at one school versus another in different categories, check out the Net Price Calculators for schools you know, and see how widely the net prices you get are across the board, based on your financial situation.

Highly selective schools

These are the ones everyone knows. The Ivies. Schools like Northwestern or University of Chicago if you live in Chicago like I used to. They admit a very small percentage of students that apply (and are highly ranked, if you care about that). This means they don't NEED to give out financial aid to convince kids to attend. The difference comes in with need-based aid. If you show financial need (and you get admitted), many of these schools will cover 100% of it. They have large endowments, and they want to diversify their student bodies. (Google "schools that meet 100% of financial need" and see how small the list is, usually around 70 schools)

Large state flagship schools (either in or out of state)

These are also typically well known. They also get a ton of applications and can be very selective - hello, University of Michigan. Some give preference in financial aid to residents of their state. They are more likely to offer loans as a part of financial aid they do offer, and don't offer much in merit aid unless the student is truly outstanding. Out-of-state tuition to one of these can cost as much or more as a highly selective private school, and the financial aid to attend just isn't there.

Non-flagship state schools (either in or out of state)

They are typically less expensive than the flagship schools, and may be less selective. However, that doesn't mean they give more financial aid. All public schools are getting squeezed by shrinking state budgets, and that includes financial aid. It's worth checking out a few Net Price calculators for these institutions in your state, but my guess is the out-of-state ones won't be very generous. That being said, there ARE some that are lowering tuition to attract out-of-staters.

Mid-sized private schools

There aren't very many of these, but if you're looking for more aid, less selectivity, and larger student bodies, you might check out a few of them. From what I've seen, the net prices of these schools are all over the board. It all depends on who the school is trying to attract in any given year.

Smaller private schools

There are many of these schools, and although they are private, you shouldn't assume they aren't affordable. These are the institutions that can give out great financial aid packages that could cover 100% of calculated financial need. They can also have significant merit scholarships meant to attract the kinds of solid students they want. They offer a wide range of settings, programs, and social situations. For the student with some financial need, solid academic credentials, and a willingness to think outside the box, these schools can be very affordable.

Test out net price calculators

You should pick a couple of schools in different categories and test out the Net Price calculators (NPC for short) with your information. Just Google Net Price Calculator and School Name for the school you are interested in learning more about.

I made up a fictional student with a GPA of 3.8 and an ACT of 32. The family had an income of $175,000 and investments of $100,000. I ran this student through the NPC of 9 different schools, and tried to keep the test consistent even though the schools asked for various other data points.

- There are a wide range of net prices out there depending on the institution you choose and your family situation.
- The lowest net price for the schools I tested was around $24,000, the highest was $52,000. Saving for college and being able to pay out of pocket is important. Loans are

75

important too. But if you can't figure out a way to pay a school $52k, it might not make sense to apply there. It's a lot easier to figure out how to pay $24k than $52k.

- Room and board can make a big difference. If you can live at home, it might make an unaffordable college affordable.
- If you're in a situation where you have high income and won't qualify for need-based aid, you are going to have to work harder to find a school that will offer other types of aid.

Why should you care about net price?

Good question. Remember earlier when we talked about some schools that might end up on the Financial Maybe list? This is where you check and see how the Net Price compares to your Budget. If your budget didn't cover the sticker price, does it cover the estimated Net Price? If so, you can think about moving it up on your list.

Other criteria that should go into the list?

Remember those other things I said matter in the School Matters chapter? Those are the things you should focus on in building your list now. It's expensive to transfer. It can be expensive to change majors. Finding a school that is a good social fit, academic fit, AND financial fit should be the goal.

II

Financial Aid

14

What is Financial Aid?

O k. Here we are. You've been thinking this whole time: "All this info is great, Nannette, but what can I DO about paying for college without going crazy?" How do I know if my budget will cover the cost for my child to attend a particular school?

Before we go on, let me explain what financial aid is, and isn't. Financial aid is monetary help you are awarded as an outcome of the financial aid process that can bring DOWN the cost to attend a particular school. There's no Financial Aid Fairy to make the whole cost go away. She's not going to do it all for you, make piles of cash appear, and solve all your financial problems. You are still going to have to pay something close to what you budgeted (or even more) out of pocket.

The financial aid timeline

Many parents come from a time where the financial aid timeline was an afterthought to the admissions process. Financial was something you thought about after all your applications were in and you may have already been accepted. Instead, I'm asking you to think about your finances early enough to create your budget, and in some instances, think about it early enough to do something to influence the financial aid outcomes. Thinking about the financial aid process should really start in your oldest child's sophomore year of high school.

The earliest you can start applying for financial aid is October 1 of your child's senior year of high school. Please do not wait until this day to read this chapter and think about your finances. The earlier you apply, the more financial aid you might be eligible for because some of it is awarded first-come, first-served. Plan to apply as soon after October 1 as possible.

This chapter is going to talk mostly about the financial part of the process. The next few chapters talk about what else matters during the process. Then there's a chapter where I talk about different kinds of financial aid. Buckle up. I'm going to try and make this as easy to understand as possible.

But first, my real-life definition of the financial aid process: The process during which parents and students share lots of personal financial information with the government and strangers at schools in the hopes that the school and government will decide they need help and/or are desirable enough candidates for admissions to lower their prices just enough so the family decides to send their child there.

Is this sarcastic? You bet.

The financial aid process is not designed to give you the money you think you deserve or what you may need in order to pay to attend a particular school.

The process has two purposes:

- A governmental one – the process allows the state and federal government to decide if you are eligible for money

they give out.
- A school one – it gives the school data by which they can make decisions on whether they want to give you money, and sometimes whether they will admit you.

Now that we are clear on that, we can get into how the process works.

15

The FAFSA

To formalize/standardize providing your financial data, the government came up with a form called the Free Application for Federal Student Aid (or FAFSA). It is FREE to fill out, so don't ever let anyone tell you that you must pay them to do it for you.

Go to **studentaid.ed.gov** to get more information and start the process. There is a ton of information on this website and in my opinion it's underutilized by parents in the college planning process. I'm not going to tackle every piece of data the FAFSA requires. I'm not going to go through the process step by step. Try this website – **studentaid.ed.gov/sa/fafsa/filling-out**. There is a PDF document called "Completing the FAFSA" and it walks through the process and every piece of data requested and its definition. It's time for you and your child to take ownership of this process and start learning. You've got this!

What is the EFC?

EFC stands for Expected Family Contribution. It is the output of the Financial Aid process and it will probably shock you how high it is. It's likely to be significantly higher than the budget you created earlier. The FAFSA website does provide an EFC estimator called the FAFSA 4caster. Try it out during the sophomore and junior year of high school to estimate your EFC prior to filling it out for real.

The FSA ID

To fill out the actual FAFSA, you are required to apply for an FSA ID. This is a username and password that allows you to access to the Federal Student Aid's systems and serves as your legal signature. You as the parent need one, and your child needs one also, separate from yours. You are not allowed to use your child's FSA ID and should not access the system using it pretending to be them. I've seen parents get tripped up on this part, and financial aid can get delayed.

Many parents freak out now. They realize that their kid is going to be able to look at the form and see their family's financial data. Yep, they're going to see your income, your assets, and have access to a bunch of stuff. Your child is becoming a young adult. Your family is in this together as you plan to pay for college. This is your opportunity to start helping them making smart financial decisions if you haven't ever talked about money before. You are going to have to get over it, or figure out how to write the check for the full cost of attendance.

The FAFSA formula

Believe it or not, the FAFSA formula is not a secret. The government releases the formula and its explanation every year. It's a handy 36-page document you can read if you want your eyes to glaze over.

Dependent v. independent

There are a couple of important pieces of the process right off the bat. The FAFSA form asks a bunch of questions to determine if your child is dependent or not. Independent children do not have to report anyone's financial information but their own. This is a HUGE benefit and can increase financial aid dramatically.

Don't get all excited because the list of ways to be considered independent is very narrow. However, there are unethical ways to cheat the system that have come up in the news recently with regards to changing guardianship of your child. I expect this loophole to be examined very closely going forward.

The most likely reasons a student is independent is that they are older than 24 when they are attending, they are married, they are pursuing a graduate degree, or they have dependent children of their own. There are other reasons, but much less prevalent. Otherwise, your child is dependent for financial aid purposes. Kicking them out of the house isn't going to change this. Claiming that they work and support themselves isn't going to change this.

Who is the parent who needs to provide information?

I'm going under the assumption that your student is dependent at this point. The FAFSA form will then ask for parent information. Figuring out who should fill out this section is not as straightforward as you would think.

The FAFSA form cares whether or not the biological parents are married, whether or not they live together, who the student lived with more, who provided more financial support during the last 12 months, and whether or not that parent is remarried.

It is not based on:

- who has "custody" - and may not be the same as the "custodial parent" in any legal agreement
- who takes the income tax exemption
- any agreements made in a divorce agreement as to who is responsible to pay for college

In general, the parental information required is the parent the student has lived with the most during the last 12 months, and the parent's spouse if they have one. Just follow the directions provided in the prompts during these questions and you should be good to go.

Information for divorced parents

The result of these rules is that there could be a benefit to the child living with the parent with the lower income. Again, this seems straightforward, but it isn't.

- Child support is counted as untaxed income, so you need to add that in to your consideration. Changes in the way alimony is taxed after 2018 also have changed how it may be reported on the FAFSA. I am not seeing clear direction on this yet from the FAFSA guide, but I expect it will be updated.

- If the parent is remarried, the stepparent's income is required to be included on the FAFSA. Got a prenup? Doesn't matter, the federal government doesn't care when it comes to paying for college.
- If the school is one of several hundred that require the CSS profile (more on this later), the benefit of living with the lower income parent could be negated if the school requires financial information from the non-custodial parent (and their spouse, if they have one).

The financial data

Once you've gotten through whose information needs to be included, it's time to start entering the financial data. Each question you answer has help text associated with it. You can reference the "Completing the FAFSA" PDF I mentioned earlier. You can also call the FAFSA helpline and ask questions. Also feel free to hop into the Facebook groups and ask, but verify any answers you receive before you rely on them.

In general, the form asks for Student Income, Student Assets, Parent Income and Parent Assets. Income information comes from your tax return or directly from the IRS using the DRT tool I mentioned previously. Assets are things like investments, bank accounts, trusts, and equity in property. Think of these categories as four separate buckets that go into a box and come out the other end in total as the EFC.

Income categories refer back to income that was earned in the year prior-prior to the year in school you want financial aid for. For example, if your student is attending college starting in 2020-2021, the income entered into the FAFSA is from 2018. Since you will be filling out the FAFSA in the fall of 2019, it is TOO LATE to do anything about your income from that year. It's already been earned, and unless you're way late on filing your 2018 taxes (i.e. you filed an extension to October 15), it's already been reported to the IRS.

Strategies to reduce income to reduce the EFC and hopefully qualify for additional financial aid can only be implemented if you think about this early enough in the process (you were earning this income during your child's sophomore/junior years). In this example, 2018 is the "Base year" for financial aid purposes. Even if you can reduce your income in subsequent years, financial aid is in relation to your base year and isn't likely to significantly increase in future years.

In contrast, asset categories are valued **as of the day you file the FAFSA**. This means that strategies to reduce assets can be considered far later in the process. Don't get too excited though, because assets have a much smaller impact on financial aid than income does, dollar for dollar, as you will see below.

The calculations I mention here are done behind the scenes in the FAFSA system. I provide this information so that you understand what's inside the black box and can make smart money choices accordingly. I also provide it so you can objectively evaluate financial aid strategies people might try to sell you as ways to "beat the system".

Student income

Calculation – subtract out the tax allowance based on state of residence, and $6,660 allowance (for 2019-2020). Weighting – 50% of what is left over

This is a fairly straightforward calculation. For the most part, students earning money won't negatively affect financial aid unless they earn more than the allowance. However, be careful about untaxed income and "cash support". This can include grandparent contributions and withdrawals from grandparent-owned college savings accounts. They fall into this bucket. Best to get this kind of support after January of sophomore year of college so it won't be included in any income years you are using for financial aid purposes.

Parent income

Calculation – FAFSA income is different than what you report on taxes (adds back in retirement contributions, and includes untaxed income), subtracts out taxes based on state, and a living allowance based on # in the family and how many are attending college. Weighting – dollars are weighted all the way from 22% up to 47% for FAFSA income over mid-$30k.

This is not a straightforward calculation. And the weighting is ridiculous. No one I know can contribute 47% of ANY dollar they earn in order to pay for college.

Student assets

Calculation - none, Weighting – 20% of assets per year

Parental assets

Calculation – subtract out asset allowance, Weighting – up to 5.64% of assessable assets left over

Add up the numbers for each category to get the EFC. This is slightly simplified but it gives you an idea of how it all works and the weightings applied to each bucket.

Important notes

Find out if you qualify for either of these FAFSA exceptions:
- Families with very low incomes and that meet certain criteria have an automatic EFC of $0. If you qualify for this, your best strategy is to find schools that meet a high percentage of financial need.
- Families that meet certain criteria and/or tax form qualifications are eligible for a simplified FAFSA that **excludes** both student and parent assets. Strategies to reduce assets therefore wouldn't benefit you, and aren't needed, if you qualify for this exception.

From year to year, your EFC number can change because the government changes the allowances. These allowances are laughably low. The income protection allowance (i.e. living allowance) is $28,580 for a family of 4 with one child in college for the 2019-2020 award year. The asset allowance (sometimes called the "education savings allowance") varies by age and # of parents in the household but is $12,500 for parents aged 50 in a two-parent household. For next year, it will be $6,300. For context, less than 10 years ago it was over $40,000. This means that similar families with similar assets have much higher EFCs than they did 10 years ago.

Depending on the state you live in, you will have different results because the state tax allowance is based on the state. I find it interesting that states with no income tax like Florida still get an allowance while the allowance rate for California is lower than the maximum tax rate. But I digress.

The IRS Data Retrieval Tool (DRT)

You will have the choice to enter your income data directly into the FAFSA or transfer it from the IRS using the Data Retrieval Tool (DRT). Because of this tool being hacked a few years ago, you are now no longer able to see the numbers that are transferred. The fields show up as "*****" in the FAFSA tool. I don't like this because it doesn't allow you to check that the numbers are being transferred correctly. I usually recommend parents enter the numbers manually, submit the form and receive the results, and then go back in and connect to the DRT and submit again. Compare the results to the first submission and resolve any differences by checking the income data again carefully.

The FAFSA college list

The other important information you provide on the FAFSA is a list of up to 10 schools that you want the government to share your information with. Most people list them in preference order, and it used to be that schools could see your list and your order.

They no longer have access to the list of schools you provide.

Little known tip: some states still require you to list an in-state public school either FIRST on the list, or at least IN the list to be considered for STATE financial aid. Check to see what your state requires on the FAFSA website.

If you want more than 10 schools to receive your data, wait until your FAFSA is processed and then go in and make corrections, replacing the original list with the additional schools. (And ask yourself if you really need to pay to apply to more than 10 schools. Maybe time to narrow your list a little?)

Your EFC

Once you submit the FAFSA, you will receive your Student Aid Report (SAR) and it will contain your Expected Family Contribution - it looks like 010500. This means $10,500. It would be great if this was the end of the financial aid story. It's not. It's the beginning.

The official definition of the EFC from the FAFSA website is this:

- The Expected Family Contribution (EFC) is a measure of your family's financial strength and is calculated according to a formula established by law. Your family's taxed and untaxed income, assets, and benefits (such as unemployment or Social Security) are all considered in the formula. Also considered are your family size and the number of family members who will attend college during the year.

It used to be that your family's EFC actually told you something useful. Back in the day, when college was much less expensive, your EFC told you what you were expected to pay towards your child's education. The gap between what it used to cost to attend the school and your EFC was the amount of need-based financial aid you could expect to receive. Financial aid was available through federal grants, state grants, college awards, work-study and subsidized student loans, and covered the whole gap.

This is not reality today. Unfortunately, as the cost of attending college has risen, the amount of grant money available has declined. So now we're in a situation where only a small percentage of schools meet 100% of the need (i.e. gap) calculated using the EFC.

So today, the EFC tells you what the government THINKS you should be able to contribute to your child's education. That's it. It doesn't tell you how much you can actually afford to pay (that's your Budget from earlier chapters), nor help you determine for sure how much financial aid you will receive. Your FAFSA EFC is standard, but your financial aid may vary as you will see below.

What the EFC does tell you is whether you will be ELIGIBLE to receive need-based financial aid, depending on the cost of attendance (COA) at each school. For example, if your family EFC is $15,000 and the school COA is $25,000, you are eligible for $10,000 in need-based financial aid ($25,000-$15,000 = $10,000). If the school COA is $15,000 ($15,000-$15,000 = 0), you are not. It's that simple.

COA – FAFSA EFC = $$$ of Financial NEED

You need to understand that schools have two different types of money they can give you - need-based financial aid, and non-need based money (sometimes called merit aid, tuition discounts, or scholarships). For need-based aid, you must show financial need. Your EFC must be below the school's cost of attendance (COA).

For the other types of money, there isn't a hard and fast rule on how you qualify - sometimes it's grades/test scores, sometimes it's a special talent or athletic prowess, and sometimes it's the fact that you can pay a significant amount out of pocket. We will talk about all the different kinds of financial aid in the next few chapters. For now, just remember some is need-based, and some is not. That's why strategies that increase your calculated financial need may not be effective in decreasing the out of pocket cost for your student to attend a particular school.

Who should complete the FAFSA?

All schools require the FAFSA to be considered for federal student aid – grants, loans, and federal work-study. Most schools also use the FAFSA results to award their own financial aid in the form of merit scholarships, grants, or institutional work-study. I recommend that EVERYONE fill it out regardless of their family's financial situation.

You never know when you might have to accept the Federal Loans that everyone is eligible for, or your family circumstances might change and you need to ask for a review from your financial aid office.

16

The CSS/Profile

Surprise! You might not be done with financial aid forms. Some schools require the CSS/ Profile in addition to the FAFSA to calculate their own financial aid using a different formula. These schools have partnered with the College Board to have them collect additional information from you that isn't required on the FAFSA. Google "schools that require the CSS Profile" to find the list of schools that require it. This form is not free to fill out – each school requires an additional fee.

The questions are also not uniform or standardized. Each school can choose from hundreds of additional questions they can ask. These range from asking about your primary home equity, to special circumstances, to family expenses like private school tuition, to business value, to assets in siblings' names, to non-custodial parent (and step-parent) information.

When you check the list to see if a school is on it, also check the column labeled "CSS Profile – Non-custodial Parent". That will tell you whether the school requires the other parent (if parents are divorced or never married and don't live together) to provide their information. If they do, they usually want the non-custodial step-parent information too. It's not enough to just say "my ex won't give me that information". You'll need to provide the school with contact info if this is the case, and they will reach out. If the school requires it, and your ex won't provide it, the school is within their rights to reject your financial aid application. Not to say they will, but it happens. It sucks, but it's reality.

You are not likely to know ahead of time which questions schools will ask. You also won't know which schools are asking which questions because questions from all schools you have paid to send the information to are aggregated as you fill out one form.

The final frustrating thing about the CSS profile is that they AREN'T open about the formula behind the numbers. There are some differences like the way they weigh assets that are known, but others like home equity can be calculated and weighted differently depending on the school. Therefore, your EFC (and hence, your financial need and financial aid eligibility) can be different at every CSS Profile school your child applies to.

The College Board does provide an EFC estimator based on their formula. It doesn't hurt to try it out to view the differences between the CSS and the FAFSA, but it's likely to be less accurate for any one school.

Other forms

You may also find that a few schools require a third form specific to the institution to supplement the information provided on the FAFSA and/or CSS Profile. The school's financial aid website will usually let you know if this is required.

17

Financial Aid Questions

Should we bother to apply if we don't think we'll qualify?

I recommend that everyone fill out the FAFSA as I said above. Many people who think they won't qualify, do. And some schools may require students to complete the FAFSA for merit/academic scholarships, regardless of their financial need. If a family cannot write a check for the full cost of attendance at every school their child is applying to, then they should apply for financial aid. That's the litmus test I use. There is nothing to lose but the time you spend filling out the forms, which isn't inconsequential, but it's less risky than forfeiting available financial aid by not applying.

Does the FAFSA count home equity?

The FAFSA does not count "equity" (i.e. home value minus amount owed) for your primary home in the EFC calculation. It DOES consider equity in other rental or vacation properties as a parental asset, and weights that equity accordingly.

The CSS Profile DOES ask about primary home equity in addition to equity in other properties. Each school then decides how they will count it toward their EFC. Some schools assess the full value of the equity as a parental asset, so if there is $500k of equity, it counts the same as $500k in the bank. Some schools use a multiple of parental income as the amount counted as a parental asset. For example, if there is $500k of equity, and parental income is $150k and the school uses 2X income as their multiple, then only $300k of equity counts as an asset. You can ask how a school assesses this asset, but it may change from year to year, and schools may not even tell you.

Does the FAFSA count retirement accounts?

Money in "qualified" retirement plans, such as a 401(k), 403(b), IRA, pension, SEP, SIMPLE, Keogh and certain annuities, is not reported as an asset on the FAFSA. If you are saving for retirement in a regular investment/savings account, it WILL be counted as an asset on the FAFSA.

When the FAFSA asks about investments, exclude these qualified retirement accounts from the number you report. Including them is one of the biggest mistakes I see families make.

Is there a way to "hide" assets and income for financial aid purposes?

There may be some financial strategies that can be used to work within the financial aid rules to improve a family's financial aid position. However, some strategies that are SOLD as a way to do this actually harm the family's overall financial picture and may not be worth pursuing.

Financial Aid Officers at the schools are savvy at spotting inconsistent information in the financial aid applications and may ask for verification of the numbers submitted. It's best to be honest in submitting your application.

That being said, there are legitimate strategies below that can help lower your EFC which MIGHT translate into additional financial aid. You will have to weigh the difficulty of implementing the strategy and the impact to your finances with the benefit you might receive by having a lower EFC.

Income strategies - If you start early enough in the process, you can take a look at the income categories the FAFSA looks at and reduce those for the income years you need to file for financial aid. As I mentioned above, many people wait too long, and the income year that is the base year for financial aid has already passed. Families with mostly W-2 income usually can't do much here.

These strategies work best for families that have businesses and variable types of income. Your family's business can employ your children and that may improve your financial aid situation. It helps to have a professional help with advice in this scenario, so they can help you assess the big picture and pros and cons.

Asset Strategies – Since assets are assessed the day you file the form, you can take measures to lower them right up until you file. Your best bet is to pay any large outstanding expenses prior to filing so your bank account balances are low. It is also possible to move funds from a UTMA/UGMA custodial account (a student asset) into a custodial 529 account (counts as a parent asset). This can be beneficial for financial aid purposes. All 529 Savings Accounts where the student is the owner or beneficiary, and where the parent is the owner (including accounts where a sibling is a beneficiary) count as Parent Assets.

For those with significant assets, there may be more complex strategies available. I don't discourage people from working with professionals to take advantage of the strategies if they are the right fit. I do, however, find that the hassle, costs, and unintended consequences may not be worth it. You'll understand why when you read the next chapter on whether having financial need as defined by the financial aid process really matters.

Trusts can be especially tricky, and negative for financial aid purposes. When the student is the beneficiary, their portion of the trust should be included as a student asset, EVEN IF THEY AREN'T ENTITLED TO RECEIVE ANY MONEY DURING COLLEGE. Trust income can also impact the student income calculation.

Work with an experienced financial professional who will help you maximize all the strategies your family may be eligible for, and that fit with your long term financial goals, without trying to sell you a solution that's shortsighted. If it sounds too good to be true, it usually is.

When is the best time, and what is the best way, for grandparents to contribute?

If you are asking this question, count yourself lucky. This is a good problem to have. In general, any money that is provided to either the school or to the student for their benefit is counted as untaxed support under the student in the financial aid formula for the income year the support is received. This results in a delay between when the support is received and when the financial aid is affected.

For example, grandparents who help during the first semester of freshman year may affect financial aid for the Junior year. Help received during the 2nd semester Freshman/1st semester sophomore year may affect aid during the Senior year. Help received in the 2nd semester sophomore year and after won't affect financial aid provided the student graduates in 4 years.

For grandparents who have put away money into a college savings account, the type of account, owner, beneficiary and their own tax and financial situation will dictate the best way for them to use those funds. For those who are using other assets, it's more likely the grandparent's financial picture overall that will dictate.

For those of you parents who can't contribute much out of pocket and can't pay your EFC, you may need to have grandparents contribute earlier, regardless of the affect on financial aid in future years. You'll need to bake this into your payment planning.

What is verification?

The financial aid process is based on numbers you submit. Schools then check up on a certain number or percent of applications each year, or on ones they find look a little weird. During verification, you will be asked to submit supporting documentation for the numbers you provided. Don't stress too much about this, but make sure you can substantiate the numbers you submit.

What if I have special circumstances?

Remember earlier when I said that schools don't care about your expenses? They usually don't. They don't care about your high cost of living, car payments, or other bills. Some schools that require the CSS/Profile will ask about any special financial circumstances like large medical expenses or private school tuition you are paying for siblings. Schools also will want to know if a parent has lost their job or had significant changes in income since the income year on the FAFSA. You will need to provide this information to the school's financial aid office directly after applying for financial aid. Your circumstances are only special if the school thinks they are.

18

Does Having Financial Need Matter?

I n short, only sometimes. Some schools base their financial aid decisions primarily on financial need calculated above. Some don't. A lot of parents focus unnecessarily on trying to lower their EFC to show more need, when they should be focusing on picking the right school.

You'll notice in the two equations I've written in preceding chapters that there's a disconnect.

COA – Financial Aid Awarded = Net Price

COA – FAFSA EFC = Financial Need

You'll notice the only similarity is that they both start with Cost of Attendance. The equation that is missing to tie them together, and make your Net Price equal to your EFC is:

Financial Need = Financial Aid Awarded

In practice, it doesn't work that way. Only a VERY small (think under 75) number of schools promise that they will meet 100% of Financial Need. In most cases, the Financial Aid you are offered is much smaller than your calculated Financial Need. If this is the case for you, your Net Price is going to be higher than you thought. And for those who thought the EFC was already a ridiculous expectation as to what you could pay toward college, unmet need is going to make it even worse.

Financial Aid Awarded – Financial Need
= Unmet Gap
Your Net Price – Your Budget
= Can you really afford it?

You can Google "colleges that meet 100% of need" or something similar, to find those schools who claim to meet a high percentage of need like I mentioned. Some meet that need with financial aid including student loans, some exclude loans from their aid. Most if not all on the list are very highly selective. They are giving large amounts of financial aid to students with high need to diversify their student bodies. They give little to no financial aid based on academics. On the flip side, schools who give generous financial aid based on academics usually don't focus on meeting financial need.

Can financial need affect admissions?

In short, it can. That sucks.

Need-blind schools

These are schools who treat the financial aid process totally separately from the admissions process. They do not look at student financial aid applications and data during admissions. An admissions decision is made based only on the application of the student.

Is need-blind a good thing? Not necessarily. Just because a school is need-blind doesn't mean they meet 100% of need during the financial aid process. This means that you may get in, but may not be able to pay because you aren't offered sufficient financial aid. There are only about 20 schools at any one time that meet 100% of financial need, AND that are also need-blind in admissions.

Need-aware/need-based schools

These schools MIGHT NOT consider ability to pay in their admissions, but they might. Schools that fall into this category look at financial data, are aware of financial need, and CAN take it into account at some time during the process.

In general, this translates into two VERY different ways schools use applicant financial data. For those schools that meet a high percentage of financial need, they look at financial need to make sure they have the resources to cover the students that they admit. This is a good thing if you have high financial need.

For those schools that look at need calculations more as an ability to pay metric (less need is better), they are typically looking for students who can pay a high percentage of the cost of attendance. They are trying to maximize revenue and might admit a student whose parents have financial means to pay.

In either case, it could mean that a student who, based on their academic merits would be admitted, might not be because of the family finances. Let me repeat for those in the back. If you show you can pay a lot out of pocket, you may get admitted ahead of someone who can't pay. If you show high financial need, but the school can't cover it, you might not get admitted. It sucks. But it's reality.

Early Decision (ED) and Early Action (EA)

Early Decision applicants apply before the normal pool of applicants and if they are accepted, they have agreed that they will attend. Early Action is where you apply early and receive your admission decision early, but you aren't committed to attending that school, and you don't have to let them know early.

It's well known that both application choices can increase your chances of admission to a school – sometimes dramatically. But what about financial aid?

It is possible that the school will not offer as much financial aid as they would if you applied with the regular applicant pool. They know students who apply ED/EA have a high interest in attending their school, so why offer more financial aid?

Schools often ask on the application if your family plans to apply for financial aid and parents ask me what to answer. I tell them to be honest, and if they will need financial aid to attend, say so. This might mean you don't get admitted to that school if the school is need-aware. It's better to know that now than to change your mind later, and not get the aid you need to attend.

19

The Financial Aid Award Letter

N ot all financial aid is equal. Believe it or not, there isn't even a standard way schools present financial aid "awards". Once you receive your financial aid package from a school you're accepted to, deciphering the Financial Aid Award Letter can be impossible. If you have any doubt, call the financial aid office to explain it.

One way to help yourself compare is to Google "financial aid comparison tool" and use one of the results to compare the letters, apples to apples. The descriptions below should help you figure out where everything goes.

"Free" money

Free money is money you do not have to pay back, and you qualify for it by the nature of your results on the financial aid form. This money is most often called "Grant" money. There are a variety of grant money sources – Federal (the most well-known being the Pell, SEOG, and TEACH Grants), State, and Institution grants.

You may not be able to count on getting the same amount of grant money year after year. There can be changes in your financial situation that will alter your eligibility. There could be decreases in the funding sources the grants came from. You could also miss out on grant money if you wait too long to fill your financial aid forms year after year. Some grant money is given out on a first-come, first-served basis, so you better get your forms in ASAP each year. (Yes, you have to fill out the FAFSA every year!)

There are some grants available for all kinds of qualifying criteria like women's grants, minority grants, and grants from national organizations.

"Semi-Free" money

Although scholarships are kind of like grants, I list them separately because they usually come from different sources and your child may need to satisfy certain criteria to continue to receive them. Some scholarships are awarded based on need, some on academic merit, and some on a combination of both.

If your child is awarded a scholarship, ask two questions:
- How many years is this scholarship for?
- What does the student need to do in order to maintain eligibility (either financially or academically)?

That's why I call this Semi-Free Money. You don't have to pay it back (unless there are some rules about that – like if you transfer or drop out). But you should also know how to keep the money coming, year after year. And if your child is one of those who take 6 years to graduate? Will the scholarship last that long? Most don't.

Be on the lookout for "front-loading". This is when a school offers a lot of scholarship money for the freshman year, but not later years. They want to get you to attend the school based on your cost the first year. I personally think this is pretty unethical. This is why you need to ask questions of the financial aid office and plan for all 4 years (or more) of expenses. You need to know how you're going to cover the gap in future years.

Not-free money (i.e. student loans and work-study)

This is the part that gets a lot of people in trouble. Despite how nice schools make this sound (i.e. "Self-Help"), this is not free money. This is money your child either needs to work for, or someone must pay back later.

Work-study

Let's start with work-study. This type of financial aid is awarded most often to students to fill the financial need gap. It can be Federal Work-Study, or school work-study. The rules around each program are different so make sure you ask questions about your child's award.

There are a couple of key areas to know the answers around. Work-study jobs sometimes aren't guaranteed. The student has to go find one of the available jobs and sign up/apply for it. Some jobs are better than others. My work-study job was to sit in the Music Library on campus and check out materials for students. It was great because I could study during work. Some jobs are not as glamorous – like serving meals in dorms.

Pay can vary. The financial aid award will have an amount tied to the work-study portion but your child has to earn it, hour by hour. Sometimes they can't find enough hours to cover the amount and there will be a gap. Find out whether the school pays the student directly or applies earnings toward their bill. If the student receives a check, they can just go out and spend that money on Starbucks and then you have a gap that will need to be covered by someone.

There's no reason not to accept a work-study award if your child receives it, but they should also check out the local job market. It's possible they can get a job in the local community that pays more if it isn't tied to the work-study program.

Are loans included?

Start out by understanding what a loan is – you would be surprised how many people ignore this part. It is not free money. It is money you borrow from someone else and the borrower must pay it back, over time, with interest. This means it will cost you to get this type of financial aid. How much depends on how much you borrow, the interest rate, and how long it takes you to pay it back.

Federal loans

Submitting the FAFSA will get you and your child access to these loan programs. The loan eligibility will show up on your financial aid award letter, and you will accept or reject the amount offered each academic period. This money comes directly from the government and goes to the school to cover outstanding balances. If there is money remaining, ask the Financial Aid Office what your options are.

New borrowers are required to sign a Master Promissory Note

and go through entrance counseling before receiving funds. The loan is then turned over to a company called a "Servicer". This company will be the one sending you or your child information about the loans, and the one the borrower will be responsible for working with during the life of the loan.

It would be great if these servicers were decent companies. In my opinion, they aren't. There are many outstanding lawsuits against them for everything from losing documents, to incorrectly applying payments, to giving borrowers wrong information. When you borrow, your responsibility is to educate yourself so you don't become a victim.

The Federal Direct Student Loan Program

Start here when borrowing. Every student who files the FAFSA has access to this kind of student loan. There are two ways this can be available – a Subsidized version, and an Unsubsidized version. Subsidized means that the interest that accumulates during certain in-school and deferral time periods is paid by the government. Unsubsidized interest that is accruing is not paid by the government.

Because your Financial Need can vary by school based on Cost of Attendance, you may qualify at one school and not another for a portion of this type of loan to be subsidized. There is a maximum per year that a student can borrow – determined by their year in school. Freshman can borrow less than sophomores, etc.

These are current year numbers, but they can change year over year. For example, a Freshman can currently borrow up to $5,500 for their first year. Up to $3,500 of that amount may be in Subsidized loans, and the amount is split up for each academic period like ½ for each semester. This borrowing opportunity is sort of use-it or lose-it by year. If a student declines that first $5,500 the freshman year, they can still only borrow $6,500 (up to $4,500 subsidized) the second year, and $7,500 (up to $5,500 subsidized) each year after the second. A student can borrow a total of $31,000 maximum. The reason I say it's sort of use-it or lose-it is that if a student skips out on borrowing that freshman year, and they borrow the maximum those next three years, they can still borrow $7,500 the fifth year, and $2,000 the sixth year. Don't let your kid take 6 years to graduate, please.

Interest rates on these loans are fixed for each financial aid year. The government can change the rates each year for new loans. The government takes a small fee called an Origination Fee out of each loan received (approximately 1% on Federal Student Loans). This loan is only in the student's name, and does not depend on credit history or any other credit criteria.

Federal Direct PLUS Loans for Parents

Almost all parents who submit the FAFSA are eligible to borrow through this government loan program. There is a credit check that will be done to check for an adverse credit history. Some parents may be eligible to borrow even with an adverse history, if they meet additional criteria.

Little known tip: If the parent is denied this loan, the student then becomes eligible for additional Federal Direct Student Loan funds.

The interest rates on this loan are fixed each financial aid year, and are also set yearly by the government for new loans. In this case, the Origination Fee taken out of each loan amount is about FOUR TIMES higher than the student loan fee (approximately 4% versus 1% for student loans). The interest rate is also typically 1.5 to 2 TIMES the student interest rate (around 7% currently compared to around 4% for student loans).

Unlike the student federal loan, the parent is eligible to borrow up to the full Cost of Attendance minus any other Financial Aid received. WTF? A parent can borrow the full Net Price? You don't have to pay anything out of pocket? Didn't I say there wasn't a Financial Aid Fairy? It sure seems like there might be.

No, Federal PLUS Loans are nothing more than the federal government basically writing you a blank check to send your kid to an unaffordable school. DON'T TAKE THE BAIT. This is a trap, not a gift.

This is a loan in the parent's name only. The student is not required to pay it back. The government doesn't check to see that you as the parent borrower can afford the payments, like a mortgage company tries to do. They don't know what your other expenses are. This is NOT smart debt. It's not good debt, even if it seems like a financial lifeline at the time.

You are not benefitting from this education. Your kid can quit school – you still have to pay it back. Your kid can fail to find a job – you still have to pay it back. Your kid can become totally disabled – you still have to pay it back.

And, you have to start paying it back right away, unless you request deferment. During deferment, interest accrues and it will be added to your loan balance unless you pay it. There are fewer payment programs and forgiveness/discharge options with PLUS loans. It's extremely unlikely it can ever go away by filing bankruptcy.

You can tell that I'm not a big fan of PLUS loans. I have seen financial aid award letters where schools make it sound like they are doing you a favor offering you this loan. They list the PLUS loan as "financial aid". They make it look like all you have to do is click to accept, and you won't pay a dime out of pocket for your child to attend.

I think this should be illegal. But it isn't. It's up to YOU as the parent to understand what you're doing and make the smart decision to turn it down. Only in rare circumstances do I think it makes sense for parents to take a PLUS loan, and usually only to cover a small gap.

Private loans

Private Loans are not part of the Federal Direct Loan program. They are from private companies/banks lending their own money, but with special rules tied to loans for educational purposes that make them very attractive for lenders. Only about 8% of outstanding student loan balances are currently private. There are a number of companies that offer them. Google "best companies for private student loans"

This type of loan is not usually listed on the financial aid award letter. There will be a credit check completed during the application process, and credit score and history will drive the interest rate and amount that can be borrowed. Interest rates could end up being better or worse than PLUS loan rates, and can also be variable, unlike PLUS loans.

Most often, students cannot qualify for Private Loans without someone agreeing to co-sign the loan with them. Don't be that person. I hope it goes without saying that you shouldn't apply for them yourself, unless the terms are far superior to PLUS loans based on your credit.

If you co-sign, you are saying that you are willing to make the payments if the student cannot or does not. The student can walk away and you are on the hook. Did I mention that I don't want you to be this person?

Some parents like the idea of private loans because they can come with a feature called a "co-signer" release. This feature states that after meeting certain criteria, the co-signer COULD be released from the loan without having to refinance. Release is discretionary on the part of the lender, however. You need to read the fine print on these loans. Each lender has their own fees, payment options, and features. Some have a prepayment penalty if you pay off the loan early. Some don't cancel the loan if the student DIES. Borrowing this way should be a last resort, not your first choice.

How much is too much to borrow?

Remember way back when we put together your College Money Philosophy and Budget for paying for college? Before you even knew how much schools cost or how much Financial Aid you were eligible for? That is when you should make this decision and give yourself a cap. Not now when the CRAZY is at a highpoint.

I'm ok with students borrowing the max from the Federal Direct Student Loan Program (you and your child need to decide if you're ok with it though). Borrowing the $27,000 total you can borrow over 4 years, or the max of $31,000 over 5-6 years is reasonable. That translates into a payment of around $300-$350/month at current interest rates on the standard 10-year repayment plan.

I've already told you I don't like PLUS loans, and Private Loans can be worse. There are also lots of other crazy things people do like raiding retirement accounts, charging college onto credit cards, or using up home equity. These options should only be used to fund SMALL gaps.

In total, I think using an expected annual salary for the graduate's first job to be a good mental cap. So, if they plan to major in engineering – total borrowing should be capped around $60k. If they plan to be a teacher, total should be more like $40k. These are rules of thumb. They may not be right for you and your finances.

Negotiating your financial aid package

I get this question all the time from parents. I prefer to call it "asking the financial aid office to reconsider the award", and it absolutely can be effective. There are a couple of instances where it's more effective than others. First, if your child receives wildly different financial aid offers from similar schools, ask the school with the worse offer to match the better offer. No reason not to send them the better offer and see what they can do. Express your student's desire to attend that school, and say it's only possible if the financial aid could improve.

Second, you may be able to ask for more aid as the decision deadline of May 1 approaches. This is because the school is receiving declines from students who have decided to go elsewhere and the financial aid package they received "goes back into the pool" of available money.

20

Other Ways to Pay Less for College

Test scores and grades matter

For schools that focus on giving financial aid scholarships based on academic merit, test scores and grades are going matter a lot more than financial need. This is the reason that I recommend that most high-income, high-asset families focus on those kinds of schools.

Also, for families who don't have the Budget to pay their EFC, they need to focus here too. This is the only way you are going to get financial aid that will cover part of your EFC. This is also why I say you can put schools on the "Maybe" financial list.

Go onto a few schools' websites and check out their scholarships pages. They may have what is called a "grid" system – this is where they guarantee a certain scholarship level for a certain GPA/Test Score combination. These are automatic if you meet the criteria. You can also see where the cutoffs are. By junior/senior year of high school, there might not be much your child can do to raise their GPA, but they still have time to raise test scores. Depending on where your child currently falls in the grid, a few points can translate into thousands of dollars, while bigger jumps can mean the difference between being able to attend or not.

This is why maximizing your test scores is so important. Back in the chapter on who you can trust, I mentioned college consulting resources. Finding good test preparation help that your child gets results from can literally change the trajectory of their college career.

For students who are in the top 25% of the incoming freshman class in grades and test scores, schools will provide "preferential financial aid packages" with increased amounts of scholarship aid to entice them to attend. Go get yourself some of that money! It might be worth considering these kinds of schools, even if you might not have previously.

Fortunately, you can access 75th percentile test scores for a school on the College Navigator website at: https://nces.ed. gov/collegenavigator/. Unfortunately, you can't search on 75th percentile there. I think this is stupid because they let you search by 25th percentile. There are third party providers that use the IPEDS data that feeds into College Navigator and create lists for you. You might want to look into using one if you're looking to start there when creating your list.

The truth about outside scholarships

Many families have the mistaken impression there is a lot of money available from outside or private scholarships. There are some little-known awards from private companies, foundations, community organizations, churches and other benefactors. There is money to be had from those sources, and they may be worth applying for, but you won't likely get a free ride from outside scholarships alone.

There's no shortage of scholarship search websites and apps. Most ask for you to sign up for an account and they make money by marketing other products to you or selling your information. That's not always bad but you should know what you're signing up for. The quality of the information they provide varies. You can Google "best college scholarship search websites" and find some resources that rank them. Focus on well ranked ones, that have search capabilities that will allow you to hone in on ones your child might qualify for. It is true that lots of small scholarships go unclaimed because no one applies. Don't ever pay someone to get scholarships for your child, even if they "guarantee" their results.

Also don't expect them to fall into your lap. If you want your child to win significant amounts of scholarships, you'll need to make hunting them down, applying, and keeping up with them your (or your child's) part-time job. In practice, I don't see this paying off very often. The downside is two-fold: even if you win them for freshman year, there may be no guarantee you can get that money for all four years, and second, the school you attend may decide to offset their financial aid by the amount you receive from the outside. Ask each school how they factor in outside scholarships just to be sure. The school can look at outside scholarships you worked hard for as an excuse to save themselves some money.

Getting AP college credit or attending college classes

One other strategy for lowering the cost of a college degree is to get college credit before you go. You can do that in some schools by being in a program at the high school that offers college credit, or by testing high enough on AP tests. Check with the schools you are interested in to see how they grant credit for AP tests or whether they will accept transfer credits earned in high school.

For example, one client I recently worked with had a daughter who received 21 credits for her AP tests. At her school, this was more than an entire semester's tuition saved!

III

Make Good Choices

21

The Postcard Payment Plan

So here you are. Get out that budget postcard/spreadsheet for each school your child applied to or is interested in. Fill in the blanks we left earlier.

It should look something like this:

School A – Year One		
Total Cost of Attendance	$	50,000
Subtract Grants (Free-Money)	$	5,000
Subtract Scholarships (Semi-Free Money)	$	10,000
Equals		
Amount Your Family Has to Cover	$	**35,000**
Savings Withdrawal	$	5,000
Tax Savings	$	500
Parent Cash Flow ($1,000/month)	$	12,000
Student Summer Job	$	2,000
Student Work Study	$	1,500
Grandparents/Other	$	1,000
Federal Direct Student Loan	$	5,500
Total Budget	$	**27,500**

Is there a gap between the amount your family has to cover and your budget? The school might not be affordable. You will need to consider options to close that gap if you want to.

School B – Year One		
Total Cost of Attendance	$	35,000
Subtract Grants (Free-Money)	$	1,500
Subtract Scholarships (Semi-Free Money)	$	6,000
Equals		
Amount Your Family Has to Cover	$	**27,500**
Savings Withdrawal	$	5,000
Tax Savings	$	500
Parent Cash Flow ($1,000/month)	$	12,000
Student Summer Job	$	2,000
Student Work Study	$	1,500
Grandparents/Other	$	1,000
Federal Direct Student Loan	$	5,500
Total Budget	$	**27,500**

This one is affordable based on your budget.

Remember that the Cost of Attendance may increase every year. Your family will need to find the room in your budget each year to cover that increase, above and beyond the extra financial aid that comes with the increase in the Federal Student Loan amount yearly.

Go back to your College Money Philosophy and see what you were willing to do to cover any gaps. This is why I asked you to laminate it. Don't let the CRAZY make you change your answers.

You shouldn't be surprised when you get the bill for the first semester of school in the summer before Freshman year. The school will expect that you pay in full before your student is able to register for classes, unless you make other arrangements. If you are paying through normal cash flow, paying all at once can be difficult to accomplish. Most schools have a payment plan option where you pay a small fee to pay each semester in installments.

22

Alternatives to Buying Into the Hype

The College Marketing Machine wants you to believe you don't have options. That the only way for your child to be successful is to attend a few select schools, major in a few select majors, and graduate to a fancy job that will make it all worthwhile.

The reality is that the student is more the predictor of their own success than the school. Strong students do well no matter which school they attend. Focusing on getting the most out of where they are at predicts happiness and success, much more so than the school they attend.

Major is only important for a handful of select careers. I am an advocate of majoring in something that will get you A JOB, but that doesn't mean there are only a few that matter. A lot of students change majors during their college years (or like me, do something totally different). At the end of the day, a major and degree is only worth it to the extent you can get a job that you wouldn't have gotten right out of high school.

You have options. You don't have to give in to the mania or the keeping up with the Joneses. You can tune out the noise.

Companies are starting to care less about degrees

Facing a talent shortage in many skill areas, companies are starting to care less about the obligatory degree, and looking for candidates who have the skills they need. This leaves the door open to a non-traditional path that involves self-taught students who gain certifications in specific areas, graduates of "boot camps" that teach special skills, or even the opportunity to go through training directly with a company.

Taking a gap year or years

Many high school students are poorly served by going straight to college. They would be better off working, traveling, joining the military, or just taking the time to mature and learn about life. If your child doesn't know what they want to do, isn't interested in the college admissions process, and isn't motivated to figure it all out now, they may just need time and a different path.

Vocational training or apprenticeship

Although this isn't my area of expertise, I have a few observations on this topic. One, I know that many careers like plumber, electrician, and other trades make nice money for those who choose them. There are some people who are better suited to these kinds of careers than being forced to sit in a classroom and learn stuff they will never use in the real cubicle world. I appreciate these kinds of careers immensely, and there is strong demand for them. Tune out the haters and support your child if they want to move in this direction.

A caveat to this is to be careful of for-profit schools which cost a lot of money, can go out of business without notice and leave your child stranded with no certification and no job, and make promises they can't keep. There is much more scrutiny being paid to these kinds of programs as I mentioned before and I'm hopeful that protections will be put in place for students. Do your research if this is the path your student gravitates towards.

Online degrees/online learning

Online degrees were once seen as red-headed stepchildren of the college world. Employers sometimes viewed them as lesser in comparison to traditional degrees. I think this is changing as more and more well-respected schools offer online options to try and draw in more non-traditional students. These are students who can't attend full time, on campus programs, and are self motivated to continue their education.

In addition, more and more top educational institutions are offering online content for FREE. This gives anyone the opportunity to access educational content and learn anything they want to. If learning is what your student is after, what an awesome option that won't cost you a dime! No more reason to pay for a course just because you want to learn more.

What will the future bring?

When clients ask me what the future will bring in higher education funding, I answer that I honestly have no idea. There are going to be changes and solutions that come about that surprise everyone. Based on my observations, I do think that higher education and the cost of it will continue to evolve. There will likely always be the selective, high-cost, traditional university system for the elite. I don't think that ever goes away.

A lot of lesser institutions will fail. It's already happening. I think some of these schools will retool themselves to meet the needs of a changing world, and some will survive. Something will be done about the student loan debt crisis and that will impact the financial aid process and how we pay for school. There will be more free options, and the cost of some options will come down. More clarity in the process will be available for those who want to be informed consumers. At some point this book will be a dinosaur.

My goal in writing this book is to make the information I've learned over my years of helping clients available to all in the most cost effective way possible. It's up to you what you do with it. You CAN make smart college money choices – without the CRAZY.

23

Extra: Student Loan Repayment

I get a lot of questions about student loan repayment too. That's a whole 'nother book though. What I will say here is what I think you need to know about repayment BEFORE you make the decision to borrow to help pay for school.

Grace Period – some loans have a set period of time before you need to start making payments (but interest may still accrue). Some don't. Understand ahead of time if you have one and when it runs out. Students can get into trouble if their grace period expires and they don't have a job to help pay their bills.

Deferral – you may be able to defer payments in certain circumstances. This doesn't mean that interest is not accruing. You'll owe more at the end of deferral than you did at the beginning. There's no free lunch here.

Repayment plans – find out what repayment options you have. Longer repayment plans allow you to have lower payments, but you will pay more over time in total. There's a tradeoff here. Standard repayment is ten years of level payments. Graduated repayment means payments start off lower than Standard but end up higher at some point in the ten-year period. Extended repayment can stretch payments out to 20+ years, but the total paid can be 2-3 times more than the alternatives.

Income-based payment plans (IBR, ICR, PAYE, REPAYE) may be available depending on your loans, and cap your payment based on income. There are lots of rules to this alphabet soup of plans, so you'll need to become knowledgeable to make sure you are taking advantage of everything available to you.

Consolidation is the process of taking multiple loans and creating one new loan. It does not lower your interest rate. It takes a weighted average of the rates on the original loans. It may make it easier for you to keep up with payments and make you eligible for different payment plans and should be considered carefully.

Refinancing is the process of taking your original loans and turning them into new loan(s) with a different interest rate. The Federal Government does not refinance loans. If you are refinancing, you are going into a private loan so you need to read the fine print and make sure you understand what benefits and features you are giving up in order to get a lower interest rate. No need to refinance if you can't get a lower rate based on your credit, in my opinion.

Forgiveness/discharge – You may hear of PSLF (Public Service Loan Forgiveness) or Teacher Loan Forgiveness. There's also potential forgiveness after 20 or 25 years of payments on an income driven payment plan. Forgiveness can bring about tax consequences that you need to plan for. Discharge (you don't have to pay) can happen VERY rarely. Don't count on it to happen to you. There's a lot about these options going on in the news now. What I will say is don't count of them being available to YOU. Plan to pay your loans back, or don't borrow.

Calculating your payment – Find a student loan calculator where you can enter in your expected borrowing, interest rate, and you can see payments based on your repayment plan. Don't be surprised at the number. You should know what it is expected to be under several scenarios before you borrow.

Creating a budget

Whoever borrows to pay for college, they need to create a budget that works with the student loan payments included. For parents, if there is no wiggle room in your budget prior to sending your kids to college, it's going to be tough finding room to make student loan payments. For students, the budget should be based on an expected salary after graduation and should be realistic based on cost of living and other expenses.

There's no excuse for being surprised when the loan payments come due. Having a budget ahead of time is part of making smart college money choices - not crazy ones.

51815027R00082

Made in the USA
San Bernardino, CA
04 September 2019